MW00773356

TRANSLATION
OF THE
LILIES BACK
INTO LISTS

LAYNIE BROWNE

*

TRANSLATION

OF THE

LILIES BACK

INTO LISTS

WAVE BOOKS, SEATTLE & NEW YORK

Published by Wave Books

www.wavepoetry.com

Copyright © 2022 by Laynie Browne

All rights reserved

Wave Books titles are distributed to the trade by

Consortium Book Sales and Distribution

Phone: 800-283-3572 / SAN 631-760X

Library of Congress Cataloging-in-Publication Data

Names: Browne, Laynie, 1966– author.

Title: Translation of the lilies back into lists / Laynie Browne.

Description: First edition. | Seattle : Wave Books, [2022]

Identifiers: LCCN 2021042955 | ISBN 9781950268610 (hardcover)

ISBN 9781950268603 (paperback)

Subjects: LCGFT: Poetry.

Classification: LCC PS3552.R748 T73 2022 | DDC 811/.54—dc23

LC record available at https://lccn.loc.gov/2021042955

Designed by Crisis

Printed in the United States of America

9 8 7 6 5 4 3 2 1

First Edition

Wave Books 101

FOR C. D. WRIGHT

# TRANSLATION
## OF THE
## LILIES BACK
## INTO LISTS

*The entire room then became a person I knew, in many bodies.*

# 12.16.15

1. Can I look without stammering?

2. Do crossed-out items count?

3. A virtual image must be remembered flatly, then sent with signatures, commemorating the location of printing letters side by side on a page.

4. When someone buys you a gift every year in December and you wish this weren't the case, because you aren't in the habit of exchanging many gifts, though you feel warmly about these friends, colleagues, or relations, you immediately forget this has happened for another year.

5. (After you send a gift quickly in return, and a thank-you note) and so the cycle continues.

6. But how might it end? Perhaps not unlike many other forced aspects of discourse or housework.

7. Repetitions continue.

8. The table is dirty or cluttered so one clears and wipes.

9. The argument in the essay is not convincing so one rewrites or abandons it.

10. People act unkindly. You try to ignore what you cannot imagine has just occurred. And yet the acts go on.

11. A few words on a list reminding one to send the gift in return aren't sufficient.

12. If only I had the courage to do nothing.

13. I didn't want to write this reminder, which reminds me that I should not need to be reminded that someone else should not need to be reminded of something he or she should be well aware of by now. But how can we let them fail when it is so easy, with a few words to myself written on a page, to remember?

14. Sometimes one cannot be present at an event and therefore needs to find persons who will represent and act out all the particulars. Find them.

15. Write a series of sentences which will hopefully open another series of sentences for a reader.

16. In other words, write a pretext for a particular audience to another's work.

17. If the work is beloved (it is) you will worry excessively about how to do justice to the series of sentences you hope others will read (not your sentences, but the ones that come after), because it is compellingly urgent and important that these sentences be beloved to the world. Try.

18. If I were able to find a few lines of poetry from writers in many languages and then choose a few to read carefully then I might think less about the constraints of public art projects and less about how our project may not be selected and even less about artists being brought in as afterthoughts. Instead I would be reading poetry.

19. When you smile the world sees something of your teeth. This may be expensive.

20. You wish you knew her better. You wish the child of one were the

friend of the child of another. But in the period known as being a parent of adolescent children, the little power one has is mostly invisible.

21. I wish I could restring it myself.

22. You have to think carefully about your choices.

23. I prefer aisles.

1. When you've made a plan but aren't sure how many times you must confirm, are you more or less certain with each time you check your whereabouts? Will you have a place to lay down your head? Try this in different cities with persons you've never met.

2. When a building swirls, as it moves upward in space, do you also begin to think in spirals? What colors are your footsteps as you rise?

3. She grew up across the street from herself, inside a museum which became the antithesis to familial problems. As a result she knows the number for every room and every work of art. If a piece, even a small one, is moved she notices.

4. You want to take them to a theater piece which is alternative but not that alternative. Not because you don't want to see the most alternative piece, but because they don't. When asking advice of the very alternative actor, you have to explain what you mean. Not the piece for instance, where within the first five minutes is nudity and urination on stage.

5. I've already translated this item, but have not yet done anything non-metaphorical.

6. Is this really necessary?

7. I really do want to reread those pages I admire in the hope that they will inspire me but I very much fear I will be lost.

8. Or I will not be able to stop.

9. Is reading the same as ravishing? Why do I make excuses for necessary actions?

10. I will always be jealous of that title. And the cover illustration. And the writing within. When someone wrote to me: I wish that I had written it / or I think that I did actually write what you wrote / or it was exactly what I would have written—I find every word unbelievable, even while the sensation is completely recognizable—from the opposite point of view.

11. I actually did find it, though it was not at all as I remembered.

12. What happens to certain music played too often so that it seems completely drained of content? Do I still want to listen?

13. Everything begins to look like phishing. I rip the envelope and immediately recycle.

1. Press a page with a complicated stamp but please don't ask me to decipher what I am signing.

2. Should they be sent return receipt or what will he charge?

3. His name sounds like a letter, a space suit in blue, a bolted-down chest, a long receiver, a rain check.

4. We've never met.

5. Is it possible to carry words from one location to another?

6. When the mail comes on Sunday, but only for your neighbors.

7. Words must introduce words.

8. It isn't necessarily a good idea to encourage anyone to be a writer.

9. Try to stop yourself.

10. They are too busy, and recommend each other.

11. It seems obvious you'll need a place to steep.

1. Give up on how busy music can be.

2. Hear another presence lurking. Remind yourself to sing.

3. An alarming critical apparatus for a person his age. If only he would not use it against himself.

4. She cries mostly in private, but all written accounts of tears are liable to disappear.

5. He said he would write, and used an invented word in the promise that is a continual and mutual postponement.

6. Where will all of them sleep?

7. It could be related to indoor weather, temperature control systems, windows, humidity, sleep patterns, or hormones.

8. Is this item still on my list? If I had only crossed it off yesterday, and yet, that would have been a poor use of time. Wait until there is nothing better to do. Wait until you are flooded and cannot think. Then run around dressed with intense purpose.

9. Be in disguise.

10. Stop waiting.

11. Anyone you lived with would make you feel the same.

12. Forgive those thin needling imaginary leaks.

13. In other words, molt.

1. Other things occur, bands tight across the head.

2. I was wrong to use a circular motion.

3. What it's really like to do one thing at one time.

4. If you pick up a receiver now it will invariably be the wrong time for the person you are trying to reach. How not to forget one's own origins? If a day is not a number it sometimes behaves like a bad animal. I mean like humans.

5. I'd rather not go today because there will be lines out the door in thin grey drizzle.

6. She looked different when she was there to meet anyone else— than when she was there to meet me. Will I be invited again? We hope certain parties will repeat themselves, with the same persons.

7. Is it possible that they'd never met?

8. The entire room then became a person I knew, in many bodies.

9. She was sorry that this year she cannot contribute and I offered to contribute in her place.

10. Faux instructions are the way to go.

11. I asked him to help me with a small software problem that had to do with filling out poorly designed government forms. He said he had administrators who could fill out those forms when he applied for grants. But in the arts things are different.

12. It seems important to train oneself to extend in the most unlikely

of directions, especially when that involves poor chances and badly designed forms.

13. I have not yet begun.

14. People disagree about whether or not it is polite or just adding to clutter to send messages via e-mail to say thank you. But I must say thank you.

15. We never used to meet this way.

16. This one is impossible so I don't know why I even bothered to write it down. Possibly because persistence is the only clear course to survival.

17. And when I do the mailbox will be full. The message will say, *if you can, send me a text.*

18. I should just do this. It won't take long.

19. Lascivious.

20. Balconies, terraces, charming streets, very affordable, more and more alluring.

21. He resists practice.

22. This might be for much younger kids.

23. Write a note of encouragement and make it so convincing that this person decides to stay.

24. Help with mortality issues and something we should have done decades ago.

25. Does silence mean I'm not in your thoughts?

1. Why divide one mode of speech from another? If you use wires or if you use invisibility, either way you will be required to partition your code names.

2. Secret: employ another language.

3. Where is the life to match those dresses?

4. The dates you propose are preposterous. But I'm really looking forward to it!

5. Will it rain? Will it be unseasonably warm?

6. A small suitcase should be adequate. Mostly books, and a couple changes of attitude. Tall walking accoutrements.

7. Didn't I already answer that query, a couple of years ago? Am I being asked again?

8. I won't.

9. I hope he doesn't cry when I call.

10. I've resisted long enough.

11. I must enjoy it or I would not repeat it. Or is it just a compulsion?

12. Maybe today, maybe not.

# 12.30.15

1. Today is a subset of many days within days.

2. At first when I look at words I see them as what they are, but after some deliberate effort they appear translucent, liquid, companionable.

3. Why are some persons born with innate mapping abilities, while others, such as myself, are not? And would I trade my interior navigational instincts for those pointing ever out?

4. I have not even begun to transcribe items on my lists today, but have again slipped between tasks, which is one reason my lists go on.

5. A few words may describe tasks (when you stare hard enough) which seem implausible, disastrous to inner sanctums.

6. Staggering endeavors may be vast or minuscule. Stand nearer or farther.

7. It is not the items on the list that are paralyzing, but thoughts surrounding the actions I must take.

8. The first item is already crossed out, and being something not worth mentioning because invisibility can be a mood.

9. Transport is always a question.

10. A small price to pay walks to a house with an envelope.

11. Which face will greet me at the post office window? The less or the more friendly?

12. I have no idea where to find this. I only know that I rejected the initial advice I was given.

13. How long can one contain lament inside a garment? How long shall I mend and wear the sweaters of the dead?

14. If I confuse my body with hers it makes perfect sense.

15. He asked for a whitish root, a sweet cone, a warm decoction, a steaming pot.

16. Was I incorrect in my search for constancy?

1. Is it because you don't wish to write anything you might regret that you don't write at all?

2. Predictably unavailable or available only on such terms as to make meeting impossible?

3. The best friend of 'predictably unavailable'—however they aren't in much contact.

4. Someone stole your name. In the novel you don't recognize yourself.

5. Sometimes you sign, "yours" and other times, "love."

6. I was stunned at your good manners, your poise, your attentiveness, and the formality in which you lived beside the bearded paintings.

7. I wanted to keep going, to keep talking, but what does one say to silence?

8. We were born together in an earlier version of a mythic city, and so we set out arm in arm, to traverse the many decades.

9. I hope they will be kind, and sometimes I wish I were stupid, lame, with no ambitions or thoughts. As Emily wrote, "mother does not care for thought."

10. Fake fantasy lives which involve complacence and illusory indifference.

11. When I returned for the first time in years, the sky was painted with fingers, pink and gold, and I wondered why I ever left.

12. You're so tall and good-natured and I don't understand those dark commas you tuck carefully against your cheeks, beside your ears.

13. The first time we met we spoke for hours about a personal death.

14. You are starting so late it seems natural to continue to be selfish.

15. You recorded the fragments of a dying language by hanging strips of it to dry from your ceiling.

16. Everyone thought you were my husband. We laughed.

17. You were out of town and I missed you terribly. Even though you often failed to reply. This time a drowned doll spoke. I lifted her and smoothed her skirts and placed her on a calm shelf. I never stopped wondering.

18. Too sick to show up. The last time we met we reclined upon cement benches, singing. In the middle of the conference.

19. Time to read images. Time to speak as we have always spoken.

20. You write your longest poem on the shortest day.

21. On the day that we were born is the most light.

22. You are a new original.

23. I wish your animated tears were not true.

# 12.31.15.2

1. The daily takes too much time.

2. Therefore I propose to waking every second, beginning each moment.

3. The new year is just an excuse for counting.

4. Numbers don't keep anyone safe.

5. Ideas lurk in symbols and murders occur in figures.

6. The squirrel runs up a tree but we do not accuse him of squirrelishness.

7. Or, thievery or absentmindedness. Where is substance buried?

8. Shall I reply again, to your drawings?

9. I'm leaving habit on a high shelf.

10. Going for a walk in sound.

*If the heroine does not descend to the underworld does she retreat inside a child?*

## 01.02.16

1. It costs this much, your walks through peopled textiles.

2. Which drawing to attach? Is blue nudity allowed?

3. Spend too much time decoding your tone before replying.

4. What is the potential maximum percentage of affection inside any word?

5. Carrying too many books makes the small suitcase heavy.

6. There seems to be no alternative.

7. A doll's shoe.

8. How to avoid hearing the inappropriate non-lingual sounds of one who no longer has access to language?

9. Just because that other version of "himself" doesn't exist anymore, doesn't mean I can stop calling.

10. It used to be a spontaneous act.

11. Your eyes require psychic ironing.

12. And your too many pairs of empty legs will not return by themselves.

13. Premonition is like this, either too long or too late.

14. How many private attempts are required before you agree to the length between your own steps, to the silence between your words?

15. Become a cloaked figure for no particular season—but to enter a newly named guise.

16. A red epoch.

## 01.04.16

1. It's much too cold and dark for such a pilgrimage now.

2. A vessel with uncountable uses first warms hands.

3. Softly make things pale, not sweet.

4. Things to place in your mouth.

5. Gossamer.

6. Sometimes I am against progress, because I don't like endings.

7. Or write too many words, so as to lose my place.

8. To be fickle is a writer's prerogative.

9. Promiscuity is welcomed.

10. Derangement takes longer.

11. Structural elements require a body.

12. I forgot all about flight.

13. Even abandoned my collection of ghosts.

14. Though I am confident they will not abandon me.

15. It's good to have routines. Rub newsprint on skin.

16. Constraints create material.

17. Materials confer with alchemy.

## 01.05.16

1. Misplacing the year is useful.

2. Pretext may grow into medicine.

3. Ignore numbers until they become secret persons.

4. Pour out this metal thermos. But it isn't a thermos, that's just an image to help you physicalize an intellectual process.

5. If you want to transform a book you'll need ingredients.

6. Read lines from an enchantress when you want to be a bird.

7. Ingest liquid prose when you prefer to be fluid.

8. A good title only proves you have work ahead of you.

9. Remembering your potency impels me further. I want to be impaled by a poem.

10. Beginning is always precarious. Avoid snow-covered terrain and long-haired ponies. Avoid skipping ahead, as I've inadvertently just done.

11. Return to certain constitutional texts when you need protection.

12. Refuse to look at detailed maps. You don't need to know the future.

13. Your headache isn't fake—but pretend if you can.

14. Fantasize that for the next six hours you will not stop.

15. All pain will end almost immediately.

16. If you are able to endure forgetfulness.

17. Welcome imperfection as you would a cup of tea served to you by a beautiful, devoted attendant.

18. Your attendant will stay as long as you like.

19. When lost, reread these instructions.

20. Don't speak.

21. Ecstatic impulse is now.

22. Continuously—you.

## 01.06.16

1. An instrument for locking and unlocking fire.

2. I didn't ask, but I wished for something to crawl under.

3. Why do some of us require a particular weight to cover our bodies?

4. Pretend that a circle is not a clock. Pretend that your hands point away from the hour.

5. Horizontal assumptions stack neatly in a corner.

6. Squeeze gloves, kick your heels, avoid or obey laws of planetary motion.

7. A perfectly ill-timed interruption.

8. Although I have arrived in person my unconscious is still making your breakfast (multiple times each morning).

9. Don't allow questions of personal *shimmer* to alter your outward manners.

10. Was I too friendly? Ecstatic to wake with no headache.

11. When I walked into the kitchen I was aware of a certain ambiance.

12. How to translate, *are you able to read my handwriting?*

13. Every small interaction awakens every other interaction.

14. Tremors, along the page.

15. Your hands were watching mine. Or was it your memory?

16. I wished you had been facing me. I wished you had not changed your mind.

17. Some persons, knowing who they will be, act accordingly.

18. Do not allow your space to be evacuated by the large presence of another.

19. Walk away bestowing to those people, who know who they are, compliments.

20. My bookish fantasy has arrived.

## 01.07.16

1. I knew that I was dreaming but still couldn't walk away.

2. Is there ever a time—with one thousand lifetimes ahead and you don't have to hurry?

3. Methods by which books may bully, beguile, or distort the reader.

4. Sure, you can use puppets.

5. No need to memorize your ideas, just walk around carrying a script.

6. A video promoting a course which has never been taught.

7. In this play, a lab coat can stand in for a laboratory, with equally productive results.

8. Sitting on a ledge in a library I realized that my involvement merely meant turning up. So I did not interrupt the young writer who thought I had been assigned to him as a mentor. I didn't say anything. I just listened.

9. From within.

10. What could force you out of hibernation?

11. I miss them and yet to be a person with intact thoughts may require the absence of all others.

12. Walking away in several directions at once, to find you.

13. If the heroine does not descend to the underworld does she retreat inside a child?

14. Which myths involve a girl descended from an all-knowing flower—

15. Then disappearing inside unconscious waves and petaled chambers.

1. Reserve each morning as a blank sheet of snow.

2. Don't worry that every word may lose you.

3. How can I read from the book I just gave away?

4. Where to find affordable up-cycled behavior?

5. Am I?

6. A puzzle impossible to solve—guards a flower.

7. So you've been asked to choose the next Nobody Prize! Do you remember when nobody was Nobody?

8. In the book I found this note: *Welcome from a previous resident. I hope you have a productive time here.*

9. Compliments as riddles make me tired.

10. I want to know I'm still attributed to menace.

11. Slight ectomorphs aren't made of milk.

12. I'm proud I was able to restate my reasons, but please do not ask me to repeat them. The fact is I cannot remember them. And even though I would like to have written them down, I am also attempting to get away from all reason. I'm certain that reason, in this case, cannot help.

13. A blow to the head with a blunt instrument might work best. But only with adequate snow to cushion the fall.

14. This is just an image which represents why I am sorry to relinquish something that never made sense in the first place.

15. I dream an avid death to my dream.

16. To exist lacking fantasies is awkward.

17. However, the blunt instrument and the severe blow coupled with winter does enable a useful merciless compulsion in my editing.

18. How could I possibly be jealous of a person with a name like that?

19. Of course we'll always love at least the word 'affection.'

20. I came here to do whatever I said I'd do.

21. When you want to whisper but can't stop laughing.

22. She begs me to stop revealing how we met in a previous century.

23. I want to finish reading a brilliant book which dominates me, destroys me, influences me irrevocably.

24. Please stop making me care.

25. At the end of the book the heroine commits a murder. Does that mean I have to kill someone?

26. With great force and noise trying to avoid this problem with perfection.

27. Otherwise known as stupor.

28. Why would I begrudge you what I've had all along?

29. The end of the episode is me killing something, but what?

30. Waste less time on non-existent persons.

31. To be accurate, it's not that they don't exist, but that they don't exist as we imagine them.

1. Being virtuous was boring.

2. Spend as little time as possible speaking to that book.

3. Addiction to fastidious preparation gives you something—I could say the word "more," but I would say it dubiously.

4. What I mean to say is a relationship with overpreparation may be deeply gratifying in some respects, but also we always admire what we aren't.

5. My hope was to become less and less prepared as time went on, like walking into a snowdrift. My reasons had to do more with self-preservation than carelessness.

6. But she did not want to take off her costume.

7. She didn't know each snowflake personally but she was thrilled to have met so many falling melodic scores.

8. Walking was another matter, the brains in her legs.

9. That something extra could be called confidence but only when it was a full-body experience, like the virtue of a snowflake, like symmetry.

10. Like the memory of something we must release but would rather enter.

11. Why fastidious in some ways and belligerent in others?

12. At a certain point the list opens its eyes.

13. Where we divert is an unnameable place, or to name it obliterates any need for a name.

14. You cannot photograph this place.

15. The birth of music elicits tears. My face opened and I no longer had any question.

16. What can I possibly say to convince him that one rarely recognizes oneself.

17. His question was normal, but he was too young to be asking. He was born older than his essential self, yet younger than most planetary beings. So he could hear things.

18. But not advice.

19. Of course I'm being subjective but I also know some extremely remote minds.

## 01.10.16

1. Was her observation meant as a critique? I didn't know what to say in reply, so simply said, thank you.

2. To be 'fancy' is not my objective. I write toward the illegible.

3. It's too bad because I was hoping we could be 'not fancy' together.

4. When you see a two-headed woman at breakfast you shouldn't make assumptions.

5. Sulking is not the equivalent of not liking someone.

6. You didn't know that you had left the room.

7. Mutual silence can be friendly, but not a friend.

8. I did not forget. I refused.

9. As the rain hits the icy road it ricochets up. Anime rain. So straight and defiant, yet tilted.

10. Your question relays that you are still outside in the downpour. You have yet to build yourself an edifice of words.

11. Glad to be alone with one self.

12. When I entered the room and closed the door I realized that I had wished to flee from every living being. Their breath and their attitudes were still on my person. I brushed myself off.

13. Open pages and see which phrases light up.

14. When translating my secret thoughts I turned to the dictionary for every word.

15. When the process becomes too laborious, close the dictionary.

16. When a letter arrives, in the form of a list outlining the frustrations of another, translate failings into fictions.

17. Show up to breakfast each day with a new word to describe yourself. Call yourself a covert friend, a grand duchess friend, a statuary friend, an evanescing friend.

18. Why are you only interested in the immediacy of words?

# O1.11.16

1. My morning is not to be bisected.

2. Only light may visit. Or persons made of words.

3. How to be less obedient? I draw the line at time.

4. Sort, carry, submerge, spin, remove.

5. Still traveling away from a moment.

6. She was suddenly only one person, when the frame split.

7. But I remembered both hemispheres.

8. Drape thought along backs of chairs to dry.

9. Is it better to walk along an unfamiliar road in the dark?

10. Poor ego.

11. Missing space travel through vicarious songs.

12. When one person requires words and another silence, yet both are linked to the same impulse.

13. Some practices are questionable and some should be questioned.

14. To arrive you must be willing to actively follow the barely discernible.

15. This isn't the same practice it used to be.

16. Not questioning where you are going—but simply going.

17. The value of unknowns is unknown.

18. Bestowing the highest value to the least likely concept was one way to subvert the hierarchy between sleeping and waking.

19. When lists became pantomimes.

20. Something forgotten or something difficult?

21. His comments, though explaining failings, were comforting.

22. Mostly because process kept me company.

23. Trust this sentence but don't give it an undue weight.

24. Once spoken I did not know how to retrieve or erase.

25. It's easier to hide what another person doesn't already inhabit.

26. Otherwise, every time she looked at my face she would painfully remember.

27. I was careful not to say more.

28. Print out the names of artists. Make friends with every name.

29. Remember where the names live. Go and visit them.

30. Travel to various cities. And to the names of various cities.

31. Once inside a name, move about cautiously.

32. I'm sorry the woods borrowed you.

33. The truth is I don't miss you as much as I miss who I was before I missed you.

34. Wrapped in a small paper packet is your carefully preserved intent.

35. A narrative you painstakingly forget.

1. Every day is a repetition.

2. A question.

3. Reverse the repetition, expounding dregs.

4. Introduce yourself to inner inhabitants.

5. Allow them to know you.

6. When a visitor appears cull skin close.

7. Step into your animal.

8. Gratitude is the breath of the animal.

9. Sewn inside.

10. It isn't just keeping company with images. They must enter.

11. I'm ready to throw away the outer objects of despair.

12. Reticence doesn't tempt me.

13. Nor miniaturizations of time.

14. A headrest for water, a kettle filled with stones.

15. If you insist morning be made into afternoon.

16. Prepare cape, glitter, color.

17. Outline lips with premonitions.

18. Write a note to a loud pair of boots on a floor above.

19. If a photograph is too potent—

20. Turn it over.

21. Create pet names for problems.

22. Enter vesseled hallways and ask—the headless women.

1. Thoughts seek rearrangement and feeling is a disappearing distance.

2. Compose the sentence that ends the need for all confession.

3. Does the person who knows your secret look different because they look at you differently?

4. Suppose I told a series of words.

5. Would words keep me warm?

6. For how long / must I rely on breaking lines, as in after the word "long"?

7. That only proves habits grow out of themselves.

8. I wish I hadn't told you only because I wish hadn't anything to tell.

9. Does it comfort you when people say about your misfortunes: They make you a more interesting arsenal?

10. After the reading, during the Q and A, a woman asked "does anything make you angry?"

11. I was taken aback. Surrounded by circumstances I did not invent.

12. Write the words "it's" and "she" and "was."

13. "You" are my best word.

14. He has clean energy. I am currently laundering mine.

15. Spend two weeks doing nothing but listening to Bach. The board member found this questionable.

16. My inspiration is leaving. I can't accept it. But I guess if she can accept it I must also accept it. I sat down in her car covered with garbage.

17. Her car was like an unintentional installation, not unlike the animated garbage we'd seen in a presentation the night before. Projections of headless cats jump into walls, and plastic bags knock at doors.

18. He infested the place with faux vermin, a site-specific migration.

19. I asked: How can I sit here? Where my feet would go is a pair of glasses, decaying food, unpacked clothing.

20. Laughing, while having your photo taken, place an apple on your head and pour your companion a glass of water.

21. It isn't possible to dance inside the room you just abandoned.

22. When you left I noticed the small suitcase, in which I'd been compartmentalizing sadness, had burst.

23. Our code word didn't help.

24. Nor did the iconic waif on my mantle. Because she is everyone, I was afraid of her.

25. When I consider all of the steps I employ to train myself patiently, day after day, in order to make even the smallest progress, to trick myself into concentration, I sometimes lose all kindness toward my idiosyncrasies and want to rant and swear.

26. Before you left to make the two-hour drive you proposed to study Polish en route.

27. The process of translation is dependably not anywhere. In other words, you can't make a map of the text you later hope to inhabit.

28. I'm done believing I'm not who I was. I'm done requiring evidence.

29. I know you find it difficult to survive knowing me. I wish I could help.

30. You are better on the page and only half believe your body.

31. How to translate that into a useful comment?

32. Unwise to revisit that unfinished book now—too many undiscovered planets, and steep time required to get there.

33. In memory of words we no longer believe—I'm keeping my distance.

34. I promise I'll never again design such pitiful escape velocity.

35. Do you know the way to the oracle?

36. Text me (in Polish) when you get there.

1. Rewrite drawings and ignore every word.

2. My emoji life has never been more serious.

3. If every night lasts forever can we start now?

4. I left the night alone.

5. Each day contains meaning that can only be accessed within its own quotidian borders.

6. Now that I want to transcribe my window: stopped, sealed, quieted.

7. Where did I put that non-divisible light?

8. A body contributed to the birth of another body involved in her own double birth.

9. Blown from trees, snow mist evaporates.

10. We didn't want to be snow mist.

11. The road blows ahead.

1. If you forget to send your self you'll never arrive.

2. Place the book in front of you. Inside examine a night of blue stars —dangling—up from disembodied arms.

3. Consider the way an artist employs gravity. What falls, hangs, protrudes? Doubled-over, do tips of fingers brush ground?

4. Place silver leaves on eyes to commemorate crying.

5. Gather a spoonful of snow. Install a delicate array. A crystal aisle below eyes.

6. I'll always miss you.

7. I began this for you but I hadn't yet told you. I'm telling you now but you can't hear me.

8. Of course you can hear me but the place you exist cannot be gathered in spoonfuls of snow.

9. In one of your letters you annunciate who I am in my wildest dreams. I remember reading and rereading this letter when it arrived, but my memory pales in comparison to your words.

10. I still use present tense because I must.

11. In public your writing is a gift. In private I also guard and brood over your advice, remembering a primal sharpness, and personhood.

12. You introduced me to the selves I had not yet met.

13. You introduced me to my mother, and instructed me to spend spring break in the stacks reading her work.

14. You set me up with my own best friend.

15. A librarian showed me a photograph of the last quarter-century.

16. The same crescent fits into hovering.

1. In considering the form of "the list" *doing* is surrounded by thought.

2. While I began with the notion of translating "to do" lists into oblique commentary, I now see dissolved momentary movements.

3. Tasks which destroy one's substance may be those requiring magnification.

4. Scale means nothing in this respect.

5. A few words placed carefully into a shell or respectfully on a shelf or deliberately inserted into blankness can be more costly than a great volume, the contents of an entire bookshelf, or an enormous edifice of tears.

6. Your voluminous collection is currently being housed in a small bird flying without direction.

7. And if the bird should fail?

8. These images are designed to continue as you close your eyes.

9. Or begin plummeting.

10. What is peril to a bird?

11. First, recline in ink and paper, a series of concentric ribbons, revelation.

12. Quilt a sector of arms, collaborative daughters.

13. Walk through frozen woods, basilisk on your arm, red hoofed.

14. The only harm you encounter is an imaginary enclosure which prevents the foretold meeting.

15. Rapturously step out of the cavity of this breathing animal.

1. She skipped the part where they got to know each other and moved on to the pajama party.

2. I'm giving away my misconceptions and hulking emotions.

3. Under different circumstances you wouldn't look twice at this day.

4. I want to take these concentrated minds with me.

5. Where can I hide among the squanderers?

6. If bullying time isn't your mission what are your objectives?

7. I'm discouraged when I consider how long it will take me to dress every word.

8. The truth is there are no garments and nothing to dress.

9. All bodies are subject to disappearance.

10. I am only putting a sweater on a book.

11. Shall I turn toward an awkward pile of prose, stolen sentences, a euphoria I don't recognize or a path through the woods?

12. My sadness is not sequential.

13. The heaviness had made itself comfortable constricting my chest, so I left it alone.

14. In my regular life I'm pretty good at ignoring you, but out here in the woods day after day I can't pretend I don't want cake.

15. We were instructed: Perfectly acceptable to set each other on fire, but only once or twice during our stay.

16. Here is how our collaboration is going to work: Every woman is an icon. In pictures and words.

17. Stand still—I'm not done admiring your hedonism.

18. Every day he took a picture of his lunch and texted it to his mother. She replied, "I hate you. Love you."

19. I stared at the word until I did not recognize it. Until the letters took part in a simple erosion of meaning.

20. I thought we'd spend centuries together in verse.

21. Every item on this list is number 9.

22. Why should I imagine carrying a basket back through the woods? Why erase unhappened time?

23. You must trust that in between these lines, others will come to you.

24. I want to write whomever I read. I want to be whoever sits next to me.

25. What is the name of this calamity of affection?

26. I don't want to get used to your absence. I trust only your presence.

## 01.16.16

1. Your face matches the floor.

2. Rake effusiveness and stay irradiant.

3. A simpler idea would be to make the image talk.

4. Verticality of precipitation is steady.

5. Place your page outside, written by snow.

6. Sentences are waiting quietly to find placebos.

7. Unlatch your reversion accordion.

8. Newspapers take your temperature.

9. How to know if that photograph has a scabbard?

10. I ate a word I didn't know. Then looked for a recipe for the word.

11. When music is wrong, text flails.

12. The death of everything arrived first as the death of a life-size cardboard cutout of a beast.

13. Then the death of a mentor and friend was followed by the death of the oldest father who was not mine.

14. It was the middle death that made me alone.

15. The other deaths remind me that death is plural.

16. There isn't time for me to wait until you can hear me.

17. The death of the oldest father who was not mine was also my father's death.

18. But I was not willing to look in that direction.

19. I am inside the death of my mentor and friend.

20. Inside her death the snow continues to fall.

21. I can find no exit.

22. Her absence is unmistakable.

23. As I move closer to the deaths of everyone I love, I also move closer to my own death.

24. This wasn't on my list but it appears nevertheless.

25. Last night we sat writing answers for the oracle.

26. I have never seen the oracle, but want to ask.

27. A question I know how to ask and another I am unable.

28. They approach holding hands.

1. I can't afford your query but still peruse woolgathering.

2. Evidence of an apple balanced in front of a fire.

3. You've referenced my favored poison but your work is unlisted.

4. The directions were all hypothetical, as if she were talking to fog.

5. Was she speaking too Lorelei or simply lycanthropically?

6. Confession to a mitten—you are going to be used.

7. Your score provoked a contact allergy, an irritant to my eye.

8. I sat very still recalling a painful memory to relieve my discomfort at being forced to listen.

9. When did snow become so talkative?

10. I pulled kindling from the frozen gravure and it cracked as it was lifted and the ice Byronic.

11. Place the notorious by the fire to dry.

12. I'm tired of euphoria disappearing like smoke up the flummery.

13. Why must we join them? Vanish. Poof.

14. Coming to terms with inconclusive incentives.

15. I thought that meeting this one frieze was the answer.

16. Am I going to stop a curved claw, a pace, a shadow?

17. Or articulate how you remind me of expressionless debt?

18. A craven nursling.

19. I observed intensity and thought I'd found you.

20. Unlike any other braying.

21. Liked for wrong reluctances, but should that stop me?

22. You are still missing, but not from my memory.

1. Keep me to the right of myself, away from unkempt foreboding. Train my eyes on the sameness of concentration, regardless of location.

2. You are merely paper, an assortment of piled-up premonitions.

3. I have yet to arrive where I am, but I'm not where I was either.

4. Does this mean I exist nowhere?

5. When leaving one source of dictated circumstances for another it isn't merely the room I miss, or the view or the being alone, but also the dictionary which would have been to my left, instead of this pile of verbs.

6. How to avoid reverting to a series of thoughts no one would recommend?

7. I had no idea how easily profanity might find me.

8. Frozen eyelids, empty streets, piddly snow.

9. I reluctantly turned back.

10. Suddenly the rest of the world came into view. Everything I had happily denied.

11. When I made up a word, by accident, he admitted he'd missed me.

12. When the word you had relied upon has vanished from your memory, what replaces utterance?

13. The form in which I am practicing has decidedly turned its back on itself, reminding me why I began.

14. If the proposal is chosen we'll know what to call ourselves.

15. The months snuck up on themselves. Nothing you could have done about it.

16. How useful is pretending? I'm not often enough in the habit of ignoring, postponing, or diligently allowing accumulation without taking action.

17. But of course that's only half the story. There are plenty of ways to be neglectful. I want to learn how to choose my neglect.

18. For how long may I neglect analysis of my habits?

19. Some plagues are better company, others easier to defend.

20. While out walking in the cold my reasons for disappearing became crystalline and I prayed that my understanding would prove incorrect.

21. No such luck, however ungraceful the path ahead.

22. Objects crowd. I uselessly order them into place.

23. One promise will transfix another until I borrow my own permission.

24. The first step toward writing the piece will be reading, the second remembering, and the third crying.

25. No—crying will dampen every aspect. Crying as a mode of composition will visit anyone who lives long enough to miss you.

26. Having access to the rest of the world (but not you) is unthinkable.

27. First I must write a letter on paper—not because it will offer consolation but because sadness where no consolation is possible may remind us we are mourning in unison.

# 01.20.16

1. Newly rebirth the day already happened.

2. You still have access to disembodied plans, forgotten enclosures.

3. My unwritten letter is perfect.

4. And the yet unwritten tributes, homages, remembrances.

5. Someone else can write a rubbing of your most brilliant perimeters, the ghost of your poem.

6. I can only write verse interwoven with person: perplexing, alert, exact.

7. The years taken to grow inside every word you ever spoke.

8. Toxic opposites.

9. Please do not remove yourself.

10. Yesterday was beyond panic, intimations, a constant flutter.

11. Attached to ideas of persons, confections.

12. I wanted you to read my mind, dear edifice—

13. When I arrived my fantasy had already departed.

14. For no reason.

15. We were tempted to recycle 'magnificence.'

16. 'We' meaning all of *our* 'selves.'

17. If I ever recover from live transmissions.

18. Make purity a vital relic.

19. Electromagnetic day school.

20. Correspondence made me a part of the world.

21. Uninterested in 'self' you spent entirely too much time inside succulence, a prolonged histology.

22. Now I can see you were severely aghast.

23. You ask why can't I just get over the irrepressible.

24. I used to be open for obscure painstaking reasons.

25. Now I have no hope, but continue out of habit.

26. Seared, punctured, punctuated, drowned.

27. You did this to me in words.

# 01.25.16

1. Protective of your future music.

2. I wake your songs and ask them to rise and dress.

3. Reading a book much later than it was written might reveal a character you have become.

4. A love spell in reverse.

5. So we go back to beginning, being crushed.

6. By various spines we cannot bear to touch.

7. Though remembering every word and the way you look on the page.

8. How might I protect your book covers from aging? It seems only a moment ago they were new.

9. Now copies are almost impossible to find.

10. Certain questions cannot be written because to do so is to admit to asking.

11. I wrote back to the second request to repeat the same action I could not deny.

12. The number of your remembrances must be an undiscovered number.

13. Calls made when no one could hear.

14. Imagine an unscathed response, with almost no weight.

15. Make one appointment to take photographs of numbers, another to make them count.

16. Research project: find a person who is able to hear words un-spoken and to draw speech from stone.

17. This person should come in contrasting colors and stand out against snow.

18. But how can I trust the outline of a person unseen?

19. Make the unseen a guardian of your most beloved fears.

20. Place books in envelopes. Mail one package to your future. Another to replace a past you have yet to believe.

21. When the cost of fuel dwindles, dream twice as far.

22. List background colors, soft applications, kindling for eyes.

## 01.26.16

1. What sustains us is often not remembered or ever written.

2. I asked him to repeat some words before bed, permissions to disappear.

3. The prayer knew everyone's worry.

4. She said she didn't mind the snow because it brightened her view.

5. Instead of shoveling a path to the mailbox—stomp.

6. A reminder that I never did trim dead insistence or delete the idiotic.

7. So I've resorted to disambiguation.

8. No, to block one path ahead is an attempt to direct.

9. Every effort, beginning now, will trudge according to plan.

10. Yet when I look out onto the snow-covered distance it hurts my eyes.

11. Dissect the word 'trust.'

12. If we were supposed to be unafraid we would have been born that way.

13. Which words to admit our undreamt worst nightmares?

14. Delicacy which scars breath.

15. Saying little or nothing makes something less true only when I wish I could simply say: we will be alright.

16. Knowing full well that to grow up too slowly is another sort of casualty.

17. Not wanting to be born. Crying upon separation. Ignoring one's gifts. Moving so slowly so as to freeze in place certain possibilities.

18. Skin may be translucent but thought is not.

19. Come here and tell me everything.

20. The type of love one may never put down even when lapsing in consciousness, regardless of the words of the prayer.

21. A mother worries her son will come home in a body bag.

22. And what did I say in response? I was so young, I had not yet been assembled.

23. What you never put down is the promise of being alive.

24. When lacking a schedule one makes pacts with oneself.

25. The post office is a tempting excavation.

26. The series of sentences which must be written have yet to be discovered.

27. Is a writer then an explorer—who sets out in search of sentences?

28. Once found is a name a flag?

29. But the place one must go to retrieve the unwritten is a non-place.

30. At first the corner of my left eye began to aspirate and then I knew the impossibility of a non-moving background.

## 01.28.16

1. My dreams were unimaginable.

2. Uncertain of themselves.

3. Outside is still blinding white.

4. Form breaks thought from churlish prose.

5. I curled my toes away from dream.

6. It curdled. I was sick and mad and changed the ways I would respond in waking life.

7. I'd never before dreamed this distance—between what would never occur and what had never occurred.

8. The distance was a lack of charm.

9. A thoughtful person would not visit this single-track sitting room.

10. I'm behind in reading headlines—not headlines but nearlines.

11. One eye told the other eye, and so on.

12. But how am I supposed to deal with the fallout from my unconscious?

13. The imaginary damage I've done is severe.

14. I never meant to fall into prevarication but my psyche was an accessible puddle.

15. An indiscriminate and magnetic region of every morning.

16. Behaving differently, you might be someone else.

17. An author of problems.

18. Not the ones you suspect.

19. The narrative one family member attends is the unlikely yoke of another.

20. Raised in the same middle distance not seeing certain streets— but instead memories of streets become obligatory animals.

21. The day contained too many moving parts, too many verbal and physical obstinate slender tubes.

22. The way she stood on tiptoe higher and higher as if to gain perspective.

23. The children continued to talk over her in the classroom. She tried giddiness and flight.

24. One memory is a mammal and another a living body of water, thus the conversation is muddy.

25. Her idea of disagreement was to say nothing while constructing a hidden afterward.

26. When pressed, she said, you and I are not usually near the trailing edge of a wing.

27. She thought she'd outlived falsehoods, yet they were mostly still loam.

28. She acted as if it were inconvenient, his schedule for dwindling.

29. I could not say this so I stayed in lockstep.

30. Is that why I dream of paleography?

31. A chill up the side of my body, ending at necrology.

32. When I asked the doctor how to prevent a recurrence, he replied: Don't be a woman. Don't be your age.

33. My tears were measured in millimeters on small strips of paper.

34. Garments could not protect me except when I imagined myself lachrymose, invisible lace.

# 01.29.16

1. I'm amazed at everything I cannot say.

2. It used to be nothing.

3. But the unsaid keeps expanding as incapacity comes into greater view.

4. If you aren't listening you still hear a deadweight in hypotheses.

5. You'd think I would've noticed sooner.

6. The world required does not exist.

7. That's never 'stoppered' you.

8. Trying to write directly from skies.

9. Ghosts arriving for visits are not exact in revealing their plans.

10. Write one million letters to sound intentions.

11. Riven is right—is revision—is night.

12. Complete a crucial segment of forbidden promise.

13. Take your time to grow up.

14. Mythic cities won't abandon wanderers.

15. My eyes had other ideas, rejecting branches etched into feathery skies.

16. Write the names tentatively, to see how they will react.

17. Your head is an object you carry unceasingly between shoulders.

18. Direct transfer of color to windows is precarious shedding of heat.

19. Wrap hesitations in small portable stoves and stow incendiary notions.

1. Writing the date at the top of the page, I realized I had forgotten.

2. Yesterday wasn't a number. A falsely dappled or dilapidated conversation was unconsciously part of my failure.

3. I'm still sorry and somewhat shocked at my own animated disbelief.

4. If only the mind would tell us, in advance, when it means to act.

5. Though inaction also would benefit by knowing.

6. An envelope, unopened, placed on top, is also a reminder.

7. And what is scribbled on the outside of the envelope.

8. We want to have them over but days are competitive with absence.

9. And we have yet to build fire from misgivings.

10. It's true the act of truth telling might suck all the warm air out of the room.

11. Even if beautiful, some promises leave us cold.

12. A friendship began as a way to distract yourself from the remoteness of another.

13. If only you could choose whom to keep at a distance, and birds swooping.

14. I wanted to begin this now, while everyone else is asleep.

15. Your return address includes a portrait of a wolf.

16. Because you donated to the wild.

17. He held the book above him in bed and as he began to drift the book waved and wobbled.

18. We'll let him sleep until the hour the sky is drained of breath.

19. He kept options open, always having a back-up as if love were a series of carefully positioned explosives.

20. But the real icon is always a child.

21. I feared the book might fall onto his face, breaking his glasses, or onto mine disturbing an abstract gravity.

22. I need a mantra, so the lovesick may sleep.

23. A list of the names of various stone cottages strewn through the woods.

24. Will I remember what the names potentially indicate, years later?

25. Where to inscribe instructions for unborn years?

26. It looked as if we were reading drunk or conducting a sleeping orchestra.

27. She dreamed I sang exophoric songs, crying ribbons of prose and robins.

28. You were alive again.

29. I wanted to slip beyond the mishap of falling things, lights, lives, letters.

*Disregard those formerly fallen crystallized selves.*

1. You touched my waist, an arc.

2. Near to aggravating silence and absent from anticipated sound.

3. A small speechless animal drenched in haze.

4. Snow disappears—travels to undisclosed locations.

5. I open my handheld-mind to see where I was the night before.

6. Thoughts are not containable, yet building cities or wastelands of words provides a home.

7. Explains obsession with form.

8. A few words on a list can expand exponentially becoming potentially intrusive.

9. Translation of thoughts, or lilies, into lists is coping with finitude.

10. I say lilies because the reproductive parts are most delicate.

11. We value our own flowering and then the bloom of generations.

12. Our continued existence is dependent on this ability to flower.

13. You could say it's metaphorical and also literal. Your flower is the location of your chosen pulse. Where you are alive. Where you want to continue—to live beyond yourself.

14. This is both a poem and a pullout statement—a way to represent.

15. Poetics are not a fold-out couch, a disappearing train, a combative rhetoric, a proclamation or prescription. Change and attention are all I can promise. In other words, love.

16. The background of my listening is trying to hear what is being said that isn't yet set.

17. In any coded conversation you can only hear the language you already understand.

18. And yet you are invited.

19. To mess up, not to exclude, not to assume.

20. I was amazed when I heard on the radio a clear positive statement. Sometimes the act of simply representing oneself seems impossible.

21. We don't want our translations to try too hard—thereby forgetting their bodies. We don't aim to be incomprehensible either.

22. I'm the last to know what I'm doing, for instance: 'the move that links aesthetic lineage, love, and critical synthesis.'

23. She explained the burial rituals by way of Monty Python.

24. Games that make us old: pedaling albums, remembering a seasonal flywheel fest.

25. I need to be in contact more but to whom can I admit it? 'It' being—the stress of the stress of—

26. It's okay to close your door because we are the most annoying humans ever, but not okay if you hate the world.

27. Attachment to a font is a backward writing by hand. Words visually enwrap the eye.

28. Writing 2015 instead of 2016 the 5 looked so naked, young, and wrong, which indicates we are now firmly in the new year.

29. A speculative space yet unwritten.

30. Send instructions to friends.

31. Finished, unfinished, delete, trust these persons to help.

32. Take care of our future please—the one I won't be here for.

33. Everyone else has known for a long time we are all going to die.

34. Definitely not a coincidence—spirit errands coincide.

35. I feed my familiars in more ways than one.

36. One dependent is not the same as another.

37. I've grown up depending on persons who continue being humans.

38. Departures should not be unexpected.

39. Yet I refuse to end that way.

## 02.01.16.2

1. Why is waiting always cold?

2. We don't have separate bodies, even while we do.

3. Worry dolls hung from mock chandelier.

4. I heard a voice and undressed that voice.

5. An unpretty picture we'd rather not draw.

6. Forgetting every awkward stage.

7. My occupation is to wonder, but it doesn't pay.

8. How much space to give another is one pertinent question.

9. How much of this is my business.

10. You could say we are a particularly close family not knowing how to become ourselves.

11. We have not yet met our futures.

12. If only you'd introduce us to who you plan to be.

13. Messy untrained lines.

14. I carefully recorded the suggestions for improvement.

15. Then deleted them.

16. No one will ever read this, so feel free to write anything.

# 02.02.16

1. That little cloud needs to be fed.

2. Sitting by a window, light entwining hair.

3. No strike that, sitting by the window, tangibly light constructs—

4. Light permeating school-thoughts.

5. A cup is cool. He said, can you stop?

6. I won't correct the numbers.

7. Schools of thought are made of light, tendrils delirious to name.

8. Snow makes a white bed for pinecones.

9. I dreamed of consensual bleeding, the exact number of red seasons.

10. Brown shadow frames, emptied of snow, made inadvertently by trees.

11. He asked if I were willing or ready to put down my worry, cradled panic.

12. As if it were a physical bundle I could detach from my body.

13. In fact I remember every single skin I ever wore.

14. Is it time to begin inviting an assortment of mostly two-legged persons to stand at a podium and recite words for bodies too vulnerable to stand in their places?

15. Order is created by haphazard attempts to remember thought tasks.

16. Purchase a ticket to be at first out of your mind with anxiety,

worry and sadness—closely followed by friendship, rubbing books all over your body, reciting loose pages.

17. When things are unbearable and even language flees, summon images.

18. Concoct and construct, rip and assemble.

19. I'm afraid that if I make the appointment I will be forced to cancel again.

20. To scour one's lists is not the point.

21. Items remain as long as they choose.

22. He ruined our innocence with inappropriate delights.

23. Now innocence is a beggar.

24. I unconsciously purchased an evil assortment.

25. But then I left the two small packages on the counter, and without reservation exited into the February morning.

26. The landscape made no sense to the eye. Small unwarranted remainders of snow.

27. It's a monstrous path ahead but only if you think so.

28. Makes its own milk melt whole.

1. Furiously forget yourself, then complete the online forms.

2. Confirm gingerbread meeting, talismans, and tarot with Emily Dickinson.

3. Bring baskets, string, apron and books.

4. Explain how her bodiless white dress, suspended in glass, is a perfect fit.

5. How notes are poems and also tasks.

6. At some point his solitary intensity turned to daggers and sloth.

7. I walked up the paper with a neighbor discussing the need to get away.

8. He'll say we must repave but I'd prefer to endlessly stall.

9. How different she looks when certain words emit their glow.

10. She wore them around her neck, bound them to her thoughts, rested her face in a nest.

11. It's alright to begin what seems distant, in fact, interrupt yourself now.

12. My goal is to keep switching back and forth between doing and being until I disintegrate.

13. The correct music never discusses your mood.

14. Instead it elevates or deflates.

15. Form continues to morph. At first I translated abbreviations into commentaries, opening an accordion-like discourse.

16. But then what was already there, between the pleats, began demanding a say.

17. Finally I've noticed that by the time I arrive parenthetical graveyards have been inserted, secret obsessions slain.

18. Hours begin instantaneously without allowing protest or assent.

19. It's like trying to board a bus or a train at full speed. Instead you wait, enter when doors open before you, regardless of where you may be taken.

20. If there were once signs, maps or signals they have since been erased.

21. Don't stop now—the first morning jolt of 'doing-ness' is like a triple espresso.

22. If I just sit myself down before it all begins, before dressing, before fully waking, and start with dreams—

23. He's saying goodbye through a door and I only half hear.

24. Could it look alright with thoughts coiled and pinned? Maybe the right pins, but these slide so nicely.

25. Should I stop imagining the exile of pleasure?

26. I've developed a taste for even stronger green shots of revulsion.

27. It's like a deal I make with myself over and over.

28. Being invincible isn't just for mothers but no one else knows this.

29. Actually the message has been sent multiple times.

30. Should I really believe she meant to sculpt my reservations into binding backdrops?

31. I was just standing there minding my curtains.

32. Too many messages not enough mind-garlands.

33. I miss you more than you've ever repeated those words.

34. The other night I began stating superlatives and you happily repeated every one.

35. You may not remember: you, me or anyone, but I will remember us, we and them—for us all.

36. You may not recall the meanings of words but the tones of your voice still transmit voluminous inclinations.

37. I wish everyone could believe: the dying are still living.

38. You are still alive.

1. A map floats above the text.

2. An idea that time will be more willing.

3. We escape another image from the same story.

4. What not to do in a lecture.

5. Wait for validating words.

6. When text itself is visual.

7. If my next thought is another facet of the same idea, should my numbering reflect that, as in 7, 7, 7, 7, 6.5?

8. Out the windows: final hours manipulate color.

9. You could not look away.

10. Drown.

11. Or if my thoughts are disorderly should numbers fall out of sequence?

12. A dialogue between intelligent statues weeping.

13. Walking in step, falling out of step when persons become monuments, or recollections of themselves.

14. Forgetting the word 'cushy.'

15. Refer to imaginary references.

16. Resistance is a mode of reading.

17. Animation inflects overt pictures.

18. From a distance those words could be anyone's.

19. They look professional, poised and continuous.

20. But then extenuating words may call upon themselves.

21. What an editor notes as strange only reveals an existence firmly outside words.

22. All textual doors do not remain open.

23. It wasn't by choice I locked every word and latched wind.

24. In a moving paragraph you can't resist letting your arms dangle in the outside air.

25. I was advised not to become a contraction.

26. To forget easily that each vantage may obscure the next.

27. Sitting on the floor scribbling in notebook on my lap—is the original posture.

28. I invert my words so no one may read them.

29. Stop this methodical—

30. I stopped reading to invent myself.

31. I stopped reading to remember my place inside your words.

32. I paused in my reading to divert your description and free-associate skin.

33. You stood brushing your teeth, shirtless, and I—

34. Stopped reading to make everything last longer.

35. Hands, wondering.

36. I thought I would begin filling in the blank documents but I could not find them.

37. Locate blankness.

38. It shouldn't be hard.

39. The idea that time is wilting.

40. What you want is not in that small window.

41. I stopped reading to look at the infinite.

42. To frame dappled light.

43. Color moving on one lithe trunk.

44. Like love for a moving body we cannot grasp.

45. But to have seen that sinuous poise.

46. Eyes link.

47. A certain recalled smile, an expression lit your entire face and then devoured mine.

48. Until I remembered unnamed locations, beyond the physical.

49. In that initial period where nothing else matters.

50. Numbness, avoiding contact, not wanting to be disturbed.

51. Yet you distrust staying away.

52. I pause in my reading or fingers revolt.

53. *Overwhelmed* is no place to dwell.

54. Who will make the announcement?

55. I write instructions to anyone who insists on knowing.

56. The hour of her death, careless as any other, keeps moving away from us in time.

57. A coldness, the body is taken.

58. Until those unnamed reservations crystallize. We do not love them.

59. We never love the knowledge which makes us alone.

## 02.07.16

1. The narrative I am writing disintegrates because everything disintegrates.

2. What I really wanted was to avoid all sound.

3. Waterfalls of sorts without water.

4. Women aging in photographs, edges of their faces becoming indistinct.

5. Conversation at the table centered around the compost of speech.

6. We were ridiculously aware of our counterparts.

7. Weak minds seek milk sequenced tea.

8. We told the tale of the guest who squeezed rice through his fists.

9. Were unable to say anything about it, this being our first acquaintance.

10. Where will I send my remembrances of your acting even remotely affectionate?

11. I read the article looking for resemblances, reminders of my own poor behavior.

12. I don't want to attach outcast documents or to be interrupted.

13. To finish reading was my plan.

14. Fishtanks were obvious wishing wells.

15. When I realize how little I've done I feel proud.

16. Not of myself but for the future of bodies existing in themselves.

17. Bodies as refuges, as homes.

18. He knocked on the door and I sleepily told him to enter.

19. He came in and embraced me, as if he were not almost grown.

20. I wish I'd been more awake so as to be even more glad.

21. I know you aren't thinking of me yet I still think of myself as thought of.

22. To love in heptameter we must reply in Poema Morale.

23. This music is the inside of testament.

24. You could not read or speak but you may receive an angelic presence.

25. Open your recalcitrance.

26. Borrow eyes from high branches.

27. Rockets bloom without asking why.

28. Though do not determine airspace.

29. Melancholia chose its own inhabitants.

30. Your hostile silence was not all we expected.

31. He slowed his steps when angry, just like a toddler.

32. The leap I asked for was a stag leap.

33. Their mouths are being torn off blatantly as they battle.

34. Rushing into the house and up the stairs followed by dread.

35. I should stop visiting your image alone.

36. Don't expect me to love any other kind of leap.

37. Yet I want to stop—visit you and yours.

38. You among fractions, you fractious blunder.

39. Of night alongside red, read and reader.

## 02.09.16

1. My house, when clean, is a pleasing still life with therapeutic color.

2. Why get dressed when I can read nonstop?

3. Vacillating between progress and despair that I might actually finish.

4. Also between company and revisiting a psychic silence.

5. A gathering of non-city leavers, choreographed kitchens, older smarter persons, mental discomfort as a prelude to brilliance, and a distant relation to patience.

6. We stood there almost admitting to having faces.

7. Like paper wheeled for miles in rain.

8. Happy as I walked calmly away in the wrong direction.

9. Insight was beginning to fall.

10. Will this translate by hand?

11. Brindled compendiums of dusk.

12. Snow is a quiet companion.

13. Quiet is alarmingly charming, wears a suit of snow, knows exactly what not to say.

14. The need to write grew beyond infancy, toddlerhood and childhood, into adolescence and became more and more demanding.

15. I used to want this something more than anything.

16. Laundry isn't exercise but may involve stairs.

17. I rinsed the dinner party subjectivity.

18. All this while annotating the newspaper and reaching for a spoon.

19. Where did I put that suffix to a satisfactory morning?

1. Waiting for a message which doesn't arrive.

2. Because the self not yet determined couldn't possibly exist in another.

3. I failed loneliness.

4. Yet this failure is synonymous with the absence of a beatific other.

5. Utopia is an impetus to writing.

6. An antidote to hemorrhaging doubt.

7. Doubt was a person also easily influenced.

8. And then the person became irreverent, as if an object.

9. Most harmful acts are not deliberate.

10. Though this offers little or no consolation.

11. We respond to messages and climb into cars.

12. When darkness falls I question every pair of arms.

13. Milk-light in photographs, taut against body, buried beneath ground.

14. Consider night a descending crown you'd rather not carry.

15. It takes all day to collect.

16. Is this limerence?

17. Every door closing. The way skin appears still in portraits.

18. I asked myself confidentially, speaking to your absence beside me.

19. Is it alright to talk to you when you aren't here?

20. You almost laughed, almost smiled, but gently.

21. And then you asked what answer I wished to receive.

22. How could it be otherwise?

23. Is forgetting to speak to an oracle a lack of effort or belief?

24. Maybe you only ever existed beside me as a line drawing, a smudge of charcoal.

25. Words.

26. I'd rather intuit arrival as continual outcast, an overlook ahead.

27. Never stop moving toward silver drawn edges which corner eyes.

## 02.14.16

1. In pale single-digit weather even looking out a window is cold.

2. The eye wants to continue to see the retreating figure.

3. We invite sketchbooks for dinner but cannot feed them.

4. Saying nothing, meal after meal, as a kitchen grows smaller.

5. Or loudly laughing at candidates for breakfast.

6. Wrap yourself in less reserved fictions, soft overtones, blue names.

7. They described fire when held in one palm, lighting fingers, a red succulence.

8. Then spat out verbs, apologizing for memoirs.

9. That's just how it is with writers, I said, but they did not hear me.

10. Too busy being alarmed at the revelatory nature of books.

11. The children were no longer children. What shall we call them?

12. Young fragments, young edibles, young futures.

13. They stood waiting their turn to be considered adults.

14. Sometimes loudly, other times without any words.

15. A glance will instruct you to be still, move quickly, define boundaries or darn your tongue.

16. Winter is the time for indoor meteors, metrics and never-before-seen fruits.

17. An elegant Parisian woman turns a cake out into a shoebox.

18. Is it safe to write in swill or thrall?

19. Her cake exploded a second time onto the floor.

20. She walks in perfect symmetry with trench pulled taut around misgivings.

21. Isn't it amazing, those uncertain lips keep speaking.

22. You took with you the heart outside of my body—and departed into the unknown.

23. You sat in the mock sunlight counting flocks of letters beneath skirts.

24. I said nothing because you could already read.

25. We'd met only in theory.

26. Did you exist, or were your threadbare arms merely synonyms for discretion?

27. Our eyes were closed. Our mouths were closed. Our third eyes opened.

28. Bells ringing in the distance did not disarm the quiet.

29. Bodies mocking discomfort, denying fraught decades.

30. Emoji flowers never wilt.

31. Each time I perked up: red blossoms, lips, potions.

32. Redness winged.

33. Ambulatory pages fall from my little dictionary.

34. Undying amative forms.

# 02.15.16

1. Disregard those formerly fallen crystallized selves.

2. When the road melts and your smile floats.

3. He asked her to be an object in a film.

4. But love for the sake of cinema is still fiction.

5. She piled her cart with heavy bags of salt.

6. The checker was inattentive to the line but when asked if he were open, he winced then pointed to the illuminated light.

7. Look up into snowy skies but you will not find the source.

8. Long ago he'd have had aunts or grandparents or a shaman.

9. I kept forgetting the name of the animal.

10. How do I safely transfer this picture?

11. An image cared for daily.

12. She preferred her own goodbye to another's well-being.

13. And ruined a superhero at his computer, ignoring his children.

14. Is sexism bullying?

15. Old bearded portraits won't open.

16. Or even return a stare.

17. He wrote the word 'quiet' but it was sent as 'untied' or 'unite.'

18. Roses tinged with glitter prolong a dying argument.

19. Your hands reaching for the paper wrapped arrangement.

20. A gift I can only replicate in memory.

21. Preparing for the storm of middle to later years.

22. Doing my best to omit the onslaught of cut-and-twist wreckage.

23. You've left unripe ruined time.

24. To be a mother of the recently corroded or plainly incorrect is common.

25. Care for a person is always multi-symptomatic, hidden, crooked.

26. I cannot be casual when it comes to non-motion.

27. I'm here containing the nothing you need not conceal.

28. I've let loose everything else.

29. We didn't leave the house in the middle-distance.

30. We carried sideshows, solstices.

31. My midwife never should have departed.

32. Because birth is not chronological.

33. But is *of being numerous.*

## 02.16.16

1. One difference between rare and random shade-grown nouns.

2. The store-bought version tasted of mud.

3. He asked if I would describe the sound as grinding or throbbing.

4. A car encased in sick ice, disobedient water.

5. Why not continue ahead, he asked.

6. I tried to describe the dangers of the party's driving force.

7. I've skipped saying how things really are, as if that gave us another option.

8. The compulsion of privilege wouldn't wait.

9. He reminded me that the subject of any statement can be met by appointment.

10. Clarity on speakerphone may manipulate your mental rooms.

11. Still, I will call, or I have called, or will you please call?

12. Ring the ruined hypnotic street.

13. The rain was green. Your fingers spun.

14. Prepared for the smallest novice thumb index.

15. To want the impossible is a promise to keep *wanting* close.

16. Which is not the same as wantonness.

17. Wildness as shuddering companion, from ragweed.

18. Come out of the railway, raise thereafter.

19. What has paralyzed this day?

20. Some plights you will never know.

21. Build capillaries in an arriving distance.

22. How many times did I write 'connectivity helps'?

23. I am captive to form.

24. It seemed important to fall in love with a non-existent image.

25. Carrying coffee upstairs, along with silhouettes.

26. Inner landscapes, outlined shapes.

27. In a drawing we both inhabit.

28. Even when we can't find hidden pictures of gloves, eyes, anvils.

29. The artist employs several scales at once, just as I'm talking both about us and unnamed others.

30. Not because of secrecy but because the imaginary is sanctuary.

31. A place to forget all those things which are said not to hurt.

32. A plain tone of voice, a procedure which takes almost no time, an admission never made yet true.

33. I am still surprised when being discarded includes good manners.

34. She said her lovers never believed her.

35. Intent to end.

36. Instead they held on to convincing symptoms, undying scripts of love.

1. I walk the sky into light.

2. Pick up fallen dictionary pages.

3. The body's demands are hard to ignore; a bird flying straight up against windows.

4. I read the hoofprints of a deer as prioritized marks in mud.

5. This translated as: *I read the prince dear.*

6. Invested in even-toed ungulates which diminish upon waking.

7. Return to a time when pavement, traffic, and cloven thought represented pubescence.

8. None of this is habitable; even the letter 'y' is off limits.

9. I don't know how to go back to not numbering.

10. Immediately forgot who I was.

11. The only freedom.

12. Shocked to realize that the epitome of all desire is also a person.

13. Even he has to iron his surface, categorize fatigue, plummet age.

14. No one is immune from this chamber of sighs.

15. Inside your own ventricle, skull, or permission.

16. I didn't say I'd meet you here, only that we were delirious.

17. Tumult made you voluptuously near.

18. Handwriting as an adjectival fluid face.

19. I'm channeling a writer who knows how to make the alphabet arresting.

20. We sat in her garden eating turnips on uneven ground.

21. She had single-handedly seduced the countryside, several cities, including every man, woman and dog.

22. Though she had not tried.

23. We took a walk allowing only companionable stars.

24. If you trust the road beneath you, all becomes easier.

25. I miss everyone who is real and also so many pretenders.

26. I'm not asleep anymore.

27. I wrap myself in blankets and wish for sublime warmth.

28. How are things different now, being ruined?

29. Not good for me—and you? It was better to be put in an actual place.

30. I pine for a photograph much too old to date.

31. Roll over fictions as if they were real.

32. Imagine you sleeping.

33. What to do with inclement immature roving thoughts?

34. I don't want to be unkind even to my worst selves.

35. If we tie his head harder will he behave like a horse?

36. He seems to be more who he is lately.

37. The doctor was very close, remarking on my eyes.

38. Almost across that line.

39. Instead of falling into flattery or alarm I assured myself of your love.

40. Certain only in that moment.

41. And so I return to that dark examination room, though uncomfortable.

42. Forehead pressed against metal bar.

43. Faintly fumbling ahead.

44. Luckily I have nothing to hide.

45. Names of pressed revelatory emblems.

46. Ahem, amen, selah, so be it, we plead.

47. My life is about to become too comfortable.

48. I have enough pens and notebooks.

49. Still greedy for books, tea, music and company.

50. Happy premonitions for our planet, and our brilliant children forging ahead, teaching us.

51. I would also purchase inner beauty and calendars preventing all conflicts of interest.

52. Do I miss everything you aren't saying or is withholding itself an attraction?

53. What has become of my self-preserving instincts?

54. Dear Lillian, please advise. You aren't far are you?

55. I needed a night off from bother.

56. Is that what you call anticipatory quilting?

57. How not to indulge in idle fantasy, or is that the best kind?

58. How to partition yourself from certain days broken or towed.

59. Alarming sounds, referrals, cutting yourself into squares.

60. Uneven stitching, a lack of materials, being thrown onto a bed or hung on a wall.

61. Deterioration, wadded-up batting.

62. What choice do I have but to telepathically call?

63. Euphoria of not knowing how.

64. I'm still in the glorious middle.

65. In the end I'll find another way to look at things beyond things.

66. Another dreamt crown.

67. I love you.

68. You'll have to imagine what comes next.

1. Hard not to interrupt a sequence of lingual garments.

2. A repeated dream of being lost in what should have been familiar.

3. Is it possible to direct a minute street theater onto face and shoulder?

4. Self-maintenance is not lazy, not for quitters, possibly maimed.

5. She promised to burn off a future of fool's gold and gangways.

6. Unable to find the entrance to my apartment.

7. No, I will not hide from negative cellars.

8. No, I will not put a wig over troublesome outposts or outings.

9. I led them around the building, then up several staircases, but we did not find the entrance.

10. If only I hadn't worshipped flight.

11. Gently clean the treated area codes with soap and water ballet. Apply plain oil painting.

12. First we cut school. Then we stopped to buy a tiny pink stitch.

13. We were already late and at this point we might miss winter entirely.

14. My best frill was an accidental twinge. I could barely tell her apart from her sister.

15. So we gave up, momentarily.

16. I knew the entrance would appear without incident when I returned alone.

17. It didn't seem strange, just an aggravating circumstance.

18. Was the entrance bashful?

19. Did it only exist in another scenario, one in which I lived less with humans and more as an eruption of ideas, a site of disturbance, a cluster of unfortunate contusions?

20. It's a sickening state and I'm glad to be out of it.

21. State of mind?

22. When a word looks incorrect on the page this is often because it has been too long exposed.

23. Close the book and try again.

24. Please do not pick at the site of treason.

25. A blinding crush on one of those identical truant brothers whose locker was next to mine.

26. Within a few hours the treated areas will develop swings.

27. Twenty years later he said hello in a park. Looking at him carefully I found no resemblance to the person I'd known.

28. Had his body been replaced with a perverse series of gestures?

29. We spread out a cloud for protection.

30. Dressing is optional.

31. Either way the farewell is bound to leave a distinct impression.

32. Lethargy, unlike some other forms of communication, has an element of perniciousness.

33. Write an ending in keeping with the rest of your lettering.

1. I spent my day wastefully instructing one sentence.

2. The problem being, I expected too much from the sentence.

3. I had too many ideas and they did not necessarily go together.

4. To mesh or to separate? And if we pull apart strands how not to grow unaccountably long?

5. Upon waking, when already awake, it was easier to see.

6. Yesterday's worry was fabricated from extinct exceptions.

7. When not inhabiting overwrought circumstances we think they aren't real.

8. Yet as I sat watching the play my anxiety grew and then began to emerge in the lines the characters spoke.

9. Did misfortune originate in thought or performance?

10. I had to restrain myself from getting up out of my seat in the crowded auditorium.

11. Yet standing close to a problem doesn't necessarily bring us closer to solutions.

12. Especially of the non-solvable sort, the ones that take their time, rudely arranged in the bodies of others.

13. The flaw was not in the performers but in the script.

14. The music was too conventional to convey the alternative scene of the artists depicted.

15. I should know, I lived upstairs from the epidemic.

16. She listened patiently while I almost sat on the flowers.

17. Her face was arranged in earnest just like those other mothers discussing discourtesy in the hall.

18. The angst we witness in our children erupts in lines across our features.

19. Is that why they'd rather not look at us directly?

20. How to know when you need an impartial listener?

21. When sitting in an office is more than an idea.

22. The alienation of so many closed doors.

23. Previous generations didn't have electronic proof of every social interaction.

24. No wonder they don't say much.

25. Photographs may seem to speak to you but you can't quote them.

26. The language they lack may obliterate entire seasons.

27. When a familiar melody revealed itself I had to leave.

1. Why do the same words I put on yesterday fall differently today?

2. Becoming one's ancestors happens more quickly than I'd imagined.

3. Spotting in photographs, burned off to eliminate age.

4. She collected the pictures and then copied them exactly by hand, reinvesting value in remnants discarded by their original subjects.

5. Her brush was so minute she knew the name of each strand.

6. At the moment I referred to her dream of the cat-husband she sent me the photo she was taking of him.

7. However, the image would not appear.

8. Too many questions obviated my view.

9. I sat down with my moon calendar hoping to learn, in phases, where exactly I had been.

10. Was my body still a viable source? Was I bewitched, or was I only noting that I had never agreed to marry the cat-husband.

11. Because the sentence I could not fix took all of my confidence I was also unable to win at cards, converse with lists or make adequate use of dusk.

12. Just as he was about to throw away the empty box of chocolates I decided to insert portraits in place of each confection.

13. And while cutting off a woman's head and replacing it with the torso of a naked baby leaning over a formal tea table I soon realized something else had begun.

14. The alarming fear of who might leave next.

15. As if you had just invented the idea of death.

16. I ripped an image of a pale hand on a lute, tore trees from forests and pasted a salamander on the gowned infant's chair.

17. When she sat down she would be surprised, but isn't that how things always go?

18. Since the image is affixed with glue the salamander is safe.

19. When I lose momentum I try not to stop.

20. Fear of a sentence, fear of language, fear of speaking on the telephone, because certain powers must be approached in careful quantities.

21. The time of day is important. When one must speak an unpleasant word do so in the middle of the day.

22. Words of affection have more effect in the evening.

23. Love penetrates the middle of the night.

24. In the morning I drank my nettles and ran up the stairs.

1. The other part of the book which is true is when the two characters become children and exit, arm in arm.

2. But isn't that the case with anyone we ever love?

3. Trying to find that secret which makes everything possible.

4. The separated characters try to find each other.

5. This writing for you is not true to events but only to desire.

6. I found you in my notebook.

7. Friends, now more than ever, come closer.

8. I'm collecting warm intelligence and affinities. Saving up for some atrocity.

9. With all the desperation that says: I don't want to lose you.

10. 'Ever' is a long time.

11. How to be with forever friends, even when separated.

12. Is the only true part of the story.

13. I wrote to you not because I think you'll know the answer to my question but because the world is aesthetically small and your poems opened my lips.

14. Because hand-dabbing words to page is a form of touching your face.

15. Even if you don't have a face.

16. You rubbed the words in public and then wrote about it.

17. Were you writing from experience or magnetism?

18. When words are performances, characters sleeping in bathtubs never wake feeling achy or awkward.

19. He dreamed of a snow tornado, kept checking the weather icon and finally convinced us all to leave.

20. Then he was happy because it was to snow for two weeks without end.

21. Forsaking school in favor of sandwiches.

22. But the blue of the sky intervened with fantasy.

23. *We*, used as an intensifier, or reflexively, as a substitute for *us*.

# 02.23.16

1. Every item comes first; therefore, your head has been subdivided into categories of firsts.

2. First rain, first falling apart, first realization of your inability to sustain any moment.

3. Record faux engagements on petal calendar.

4. And secret abbreviations in reptilian book.

5. Forced to escort time, but not to spend it, not to get to know your own whereabouts.

6. First I held fistfuls as I washed opportune vessels and drove silent bodies affixed to phones.

7. Then I was forced to carry this partitioned head, an office mostly given over to pressure.

8. Just when it might be plausible to pay attention.

9. Intentions grew cold.

10. I spent my time not feeling worse than I already did.

11. At least I tried to believe that remaining suspect was a benefit.

12. I kept putting off finding one of my missing faces.

13. But this all sounds disastrous and that's not how you make me feign.

14. It's just that certain days one is beholden, forced to wait.

15. To be sometimes unwell is a symptom of living.

16. White skies had nothing to say to me now.

17. Blankness was still hopeful paper.

18. Maybe it only seems like we are getting nowhere.

19. I copied lines to provide myself a project.

20. Sent reminders: to sleep and wake, to come out of my document.

21. I wrote a summary of what I'd prefer to forget.

22. How much was social, and how much miserly?

23. Hiding was unconscious, a protective burrowing.

24. When asked about natural predators.

25. I could only say: time.

1. She went outside to make a bargain.

2. With an entity.

3. She did not believe in.

4. A series of gestures, a corner of footsteps.

5. Arms lift, fan, fold.

6. We admired her failed wisp, attempts to make fire.

7. Made peace with "representability," or reprehensible dishevel-ment.

8. Enjoyed chance misspellings and eagerly welcomed misreadings.

9. The spot on my shoulder erased hurts more than the one on my face.

10. Because faces don't wear sleeves.

11. To see a person not desperate to be alone was a novelty.

12. Everyone wanted to take you home.

13. When I walked into the room several people came up to me and said, so you are going to take X home. As if I'd won a prize.

14. But your friendship is something much deeper than talent or love-liness.

15. We got onto the euphoria highway with no intent to exit.

16. Why didn't I go with her through a series of revolving paintings on raindrops?

17. If I had I would never have seen her entering the paintings.

18. The difficulties in saying goodbye mouthed headaches.

19. The headache as a monument to anticipating your arrival, and later, missing you.

20. To prepare oneself for too many events at once is the same as wearing every expression simultaneously.

21. We need space between our faces and words.

22. A breathing confluence.

23. Or the face melts, fails to annunciate each note.

24. Your prescription flutters; nothing is clear.

25. Or is that only glass fogging?

26. The mechanism of the eye has no belief.

27. Instead it operates like a series of locks.

28. Like a messenger transporting upside-down images.

29. Scroll back and see where you left your upright magnifying per-spective.

30. Which stage were you scouring with purpose?

31. When did friendship become a definite article placed deliberately inside each town?

32. Speed along inside a warm and well-lit train.

33. What is speed when motion is interior?

34. I don't ever want to stop what has never begun.

35. That mist we call pale glitter.

36. A vernix smothering skin also illuminates.

37. Like the usefulness of water adopted by hands.

1. My days ran away like innocent questions.

2. I wondered when I might steady grain against wind.

3. Why radio severe-weather alerts waver, as if their voices were not human.

4. Water is rising, trees are falling, color is kept from eyes.

5. How could we not have already discussed collage as the all-purpose uniform of lost futures?

6. Do I want to expend careworn areas hauling baskets of soiled delight?

7. You did not promise to close doors correctly, nor would you step lightly or run a thin stream for ablutions.

8. You were tired before night but not compelled. As if the bed were surrounded by water.

9. The storm took all of our inhibitions and flung them at the glass.

10. We remained electric.

11. A few words quelled unspoken fears.

12. Unthinkable that the quotidian ends.

13. He comforted himself wondering who might miss him, as he took his cough to bed.

14. You did not promise intermediary music.

15. Left to your own devices you would lower yourself below darkness, then raise yourself up above visibility.

16. After a few months of roving they wondered how to become stationary.

17. When taking a walk with persons who fluctuate in age—one minute five, another seventy-four—we wondered about appropriate footwear.

18. I went to the conference with only one outfit: top mast, short skitter, white viral shock waves.

19. My task was to connect many computers in a sterile orifice.

20. J was a baby, crying. When I heard the news, that he had become an infant, I wondered when this might have happened. Then rushed to pick him up.

21. In the morning his color was off. His throat hurt. He wasn't faking.

22. I allowed him one hour if he promised not to beg for more.

23. Beggar, I accused him, as he went down the stairs.

24. It's as if the conference has already begun. The hours rush from one to another, bumping into each other in their eagerness to be elsewhere.

25. Stillness is an action.

26. Kissing precisely in the center of the storm. You collapsed. I danced.

27. Later, when I was exhausted you asked, why aren't you dancing?

28. Life amid tall trees is a way to ponder maturity and also reserve.

29. They will not deliberately stand near or rub against you.

30. This type of contagion can only be imagined.

31. The imaginary may lead us on.

32. Don't visualize water rising any higher, branches strewn about the yard.

33. A friend collects fallen enthusiasms, then returns them.

34. It may take a long time for worry to turn.

35. Become kindling.

1. I could throw almost everything away.

2. Take whatever you want; it's almost spring.

3. Lightness remembered even on numb days.

4. We begin to resemble a generation we thought was only a suggestion.

5. Not an obligatory waving.

6. Upon waking he put his pelvis back into place in one swift, simple motion.

7. First lie on the ground. Find horizontal will.

8. I set to work scrubbing floors, each one stacked upon the next.

9. Like a seven-layer nightmare.

10. I don't know how to give you just a corner, just a sliver, half of one sleeve.

11. We were at the happiest place on earth but could only stay for one minute.

12. We were to meet at the Met but you walked right past me and went up the stairs.

13. Were you in such a hurry you could not stop to say hello?

14. I'd rather think you were too famous to stop.

15. They were going to hang you on the wall.

16. On the train all of the mothers are saying, 'yes we'll do that even though daddy wouldn't like it.'

17. Secrets (from daddy) o we have thousands.

18. Secret toilet training for our children.

19. I woke with eyes pasted shut.

20. Heard a news report about our sanatorium planet.

21. Don't forget to put that three-day headache on the calendar, backdated.

22. Keep track of lunar overload.

23. How much of our time do we spend hostages to bodies once loyal?

24. In the future, when I have a stupid job.

25. My accountant's office was once my synagogue.

26. I justified purchasing the flowers because they remind me of your mother.

27. Because arranging them before the guests arrive will calm me.

28. Because we all deserve color.

29. The tulips were obvious and the hyacinths are a play about Oscar Wilde.

30. Certain scents are psychotropic.

31. Cheaper than going out to dinner.

32. We pretend to be in Japan.

33. Monikers don't grow on treble clef.

34. We need new inventions.

35. When she confessed he had always treated her as a nuisance I saw one half of a couple detached, a face pulled and dropped.

36. Clouds moving quickly across the surface of busy ethereal streets.

37. To certain futures I don't mind saying goodbye.

**02.27.16**

1. Your words accompany me.
2. A letter is no different.
3. An embrace is the same in both directions.
4. Otherwise you wouldn't.
5. Wonder whose arms are whose.
6. We recall the days when anyplace would do, behind a clock tower, an open field, a ladder leading up to a loft.
7. The first new bed we ever bought, flopping full force onto our backs, babies strapped to our fronts.
8. They thought they would never get rid of us.
9. When the restaurateurs saw us coming they put a drop cloth under the table.
10. And why shouldn't they?
11. Having babies is a messy pastime.
12. It won't last.
13. Like a film projected on walls late at night.
14. Terraces inside eyes have grown gardens.

## 02.28.16

1. We are hewn of the bones of others.

2. No architecture more alluring.

3. Necessary tools are not always at hand.

4. Even more pressing is resistance.

5. We get to know ourselves without trying.

6. Every scene enacted, minuscule shots of sunlight

7. Contrary to common design it's not all collectible.

8. Like a personality talks on and on.

9. Which of the unbearable guests was your absolute favorite?

10. The parents of our problems disheveled in rain.

11. We protect ourselves by forgetting dreams.

12. A man with a gun came in through the patio doors.

13. I non-chalantly walked out the front door to call 911.

14. Can one abandon what no longer exists?

15. Laugh along with me a little.

16. She insisted on the superiority of her trauma.

17. "The Invasion of the Golobolinks," "Paula, Jean, and the Bear that Led the Way," "The Nothing Book."

18. Do any of these early works still exist?

19. Making a book bound with wrapped cardboard covers, choosing the purple paisley fabric, stitching pages together.

20. The Golobolinks were easy to track because their footprints were round and distinctly striped red, purple and yellow.

21. The teacher wrote only one word on the board, "Golobolinks."

22. It seemed obvious they were creatures from outer space.

23. Content, I began to draw.

24. The idea of writing with no plan saved me.

25. The guests assured us our city had no decent food.

26. When she entered a "room of her own" she gasped.

27. I woke afraid of the man with the gun.

28. How to tend to the bodies of dreams?

29. We care for our cares more than we should.

30. A warm message arrives from a former purpose.

31. Should I spend less time with your absence?

32. A long escrow for an empty pit.

33. She repeated a story which made her alone.

34. My youngest untruth with me asleep on the floor.

35. At a loud hotel after the dissociated shooting.

36. When I walked out the front door I was in a different street attached to a previous family home.

37. Orange trees, and a driveway lined with pansies.

38. The home of a talented wreckage is not the same as the street looking back.

39. Every memory removed from pod or husk.

40. As usual the dream was a portal. The door was a portal. Death was a portal.

41. Where were we when we woke up? Which city?

42. Look: beds, blankets! We don't have to sleep on the floor!

43. Were we unable to note resources right in front of us?

44. Or is it that we could not clearly see the borders of any room, body, or object?

45. What is sight?

46. Was I waiting for the dead to speak to me?

47. Again? If we place our bodies in the correct circumstance (the dark, the cold, abandonment) will you come back?

48. Who was in the house when the man entered with the gun?

49. I saw him running down the street and was afraid he would recognize me, but of course this was impossible. He'd never seen me.

50. Who were you when you weren't yourself?

# 02.29.16

1. On my way to meet you for dinner at the conference I noted some participants stayed not in hotel rooms but along the cliff face, the bluff, tucked into each other's skins, overlooking the ocean.

2. My amazement was met with mockery.

3. Practicing yoga under apple trees, then cooking apples, in the dark in a pot out-of-doors. All part of the conference.

4. And because we had spoken earlier in the day and planned to meet I had to finish my concoction and find you in the town, so missed the tent gatherings and midnight performances.

5. I found a ride to the one bad restaurant where I was asked whom I was meeting.

6. My confidence flagged. Could I say aloud, I was going to meet you?

7. I remembered only then, your being dead.

8. But we had spoken that day hadn't we?

9. I decided to call a very close accomplice.

10. If I were to insert names you could only read this one way.

11. My accomplice did not answer. Instead it was my ailing father who cannot remember words. He hummed or moaned.

12. I grew desperate.

13. There is no ending.

14. I only remembered being a fragment, a garment, an ancillary.

15. Certainly we are still going to meet, but are you alive?

16. Don't I believe you exist instead of dying further each day?

17. The urge to stay close to home is an ingrown remedy.

18. Should I hit send or is it like hiccups or spasms?

19. We don't want to rush even illness or pains.

20. When finished do we open another argument and walk on?

21. Most people would say nothing.

22. But I'm not fluent—in the art of unresponsive correspondences.

*I changed the color of my ink each time I died.*

## 03.01.16

1. I'm thrilled to hear from you even though your last communication was leaden and accusatory.

2. I don't have time for another no-frills, high-maintenance fright.

3. Still, I miss your damaged corona, your unkempt words, your willingness to rip into what no one else perceives.

4. Finally I have contracted the disease that everyone else in my family already has.

5. A ghost put the milk in the cupboard.

6. Sorry to hear about the weather.

7. I send you this virtual sunray, even though I'm more conversant with the moon.

8. Yes, I will be at that conference, but such a gathering is the best place for mismatched duels.

9. Pretend it's only my mirage passing through frenetic halls.

10. Yes, that's insight throbbing.

11. Nothing personal, except affection driven much too quickly.

12. Considering traffic patterns and recent dreams I'd say we have a two-thousand percent chance of collision.

13. A game in which you stare at a pixelated image of the ocean.

14. Drop by drop fills an antechamber.

15. When you collect enough water to make a tidal wave, which floods your room, you win.

16. You will receive treasure, in the form of golden coins.

17. A global-warming scenario which makes as much sense as the current political climate.

18. Mesmerized, I put my device down on your grandmother's buffet.

19. Only as we drove away did I realize that her buffet was located on a busy street.

20. Should we go back, you asked?

21. It isn't so much that our words were dormant, inappropriate.

22. The effect was to take charm and escort it out.

23. Along with defining moments.

24. Resuscitated secrets.

1. I finally have an actual background behind me.

2. All beige mist clouds and auditory monuments.

3. On second thought let's gather anything but onlookers.

4. Less disaster, more see-through pageants.

5. Why they did not exchange relevant wavelengths we'll never know.

6. Your voice crests and brushes the tops of trees before crashing at my feet.

7. Did you expect me to gather your recognition in my arms along with linens?

8. Her first expert rendering was born in open fathoms.

9. No document exists to check what comes next.

10. Advice to myself: end early, cut the remaining splinters, your entire head stacks higher.

11. Your neck has so much work and so little time.

12. Stand up straight to make room for lungs.

13. Write letters like drawing breath, constant stream of permissions.

14. It doesn't matter if anyone answers.

15. Hard not to check over and over.

16. When the message arrived I thought I would burst, but a few hours later I was standing in line behind every woe.

17. No reason to be vigilant to the extent that you never get to pleasure.

18. That's why I'm arguing with myself about want.

19. You have to believe in *enough*.

20. Your main resource is yourself—sylph of unknown origin.

21. For instance, that virtual sunray may be invisible in thunder, but I sent it directly inside your body.

22. Hold up one palm toward the window.

23. Even in weak light you can access intuitive sources.

24. If you think the ivy leaves climbing up the bare trunk are waving, they probably are.

25. If you think the wind was sent for that exact purpose, to move you, you are not any worse off in assuming fanciful points of reference.

26. Why not be in conversation with elements?

27. Nurse tree-spine, leaf-hands, unguent-heart.

1. Before I could begin to recover.

2. I'd already made up a story of survival.

3. I think of her, ice against her breast.

4. The reality of an arrangement of tulips, light changing.

5. Was the biopsy necessary?

6. I promise myself it will all be in vain.

7. Dropping off my boys before their performance, so proud I could throw up.

8. When did they become clocks?

9. Who lifted them up by the crowns of their heads?

10. Who made their limbs long and their faces sedulous?

11. While we talked on the phone about Iceland I made dinner.

12. Moss-flavored ice cream and langoustine.

13. Simultaneously seeing pictures of the northern lights and reading the poems you'd not yet written.

## 03.03.16

1. By my count there were thirty-three days in the month.

2. I tried leaving your face on my desk but it was dangerous.

3. Even your eyes I knew would not last as oracles.

4. She asked if I'd seen any coltsfoot: groundsel, of the daisy tribe.

5. The cold was such a child he stopped walking.

6. I think the woman sitting behind me in the auditorium is going to cry.

7. Something about classrooms and an utter lack of process.

8. The day was an imposter.

9. I lay in bed and held your eyes over mine.

10. The cover of a book did not blink.

11. But stared.

12. Does a book see?

13. I could not make out the dedication.

14. We write each other into our books.

15. Or, we are instructed to do so by friends in mourning.

16. Forever was a euphemism.

17. The wish fulfillment of "for."

18. How did we conjure "ever"?

19. I carry this notebook and the book I am reading.

20. Whether or not I will have time to enter, these objects remind me ineffably.

21. Now I am free to pore over pages and be tired tomorrow.

22. To be alone at night is a different cadence than by day.

23. The pleasure of these words is in inscribing them to you.

24. Without any discussion we agreed which affectionate names we would use.

25. Then consistently we repeated these same phrases on paper.

26. Parting is the end of every page and meeting is the next.

27. What are the effects of sleeping with a notebook on the bed?

28. I changed the color of my ink each time I died.

29. I turned around but could not meet myself easily.

30. For the same reason we enjoy reading about films we'd rather not see, books we have no intention of reading.

## 03.04.16

1. The snowdrops were confused.
2. Willfully I turned off my electronic future and began by hand.
3. If I spill myself out the letters themselves appear helpless.
4. Yet they are solidity.
5. Are words actually persons?
6. Is that the only static truth?
7. A hardbound book we can draw in.
8. The time looked all the same.
9. Why is one stream of quiet different from another?
10. You disappeared or spilled like darkness, fanned out around me.
11. Cascades of slippery opaque.
12. Each icon departs with one incomplete action or instinct.
13. The definition of bereft.
14. One more day I'll allow nonsense.
15. Your face from afar disjointing.
16. Help me with my thoughts please.
17. Bring paper.
18. If the quality of your test results were completely reliant on fruit and candy.
19. Didn't Emerson say fruits and flowers are the best gifts?
20. Carefully I unpacked the day.
21. Space is an entity not just an idea.

22. Motion of the moon recorded in a bucket.

23. When I left the studio I contained something I did not have when I arrived.

24. Not space and time ripped apart, but woven together.

25. We love the future because we believe it will be ours.

26. Put your anxiety to work.

27. I want to be less of myself.

28. Can you help me arrange to see less?

29. Repeat this song: Whatever I had or did not have—is yours.

## 03.07.16

1. The minute one leaves the other wakes or enters.

2. We call this *interruptus promenade*.

3. How adeptly can you partition: doors opening, objects landing, hunger?

4. All stacked requests for milk were blank.

5. Reservations for your psyche arranged without consent.

6. Your choices are as follows: ignorance, panic, pain.

7. No, that can't be right.

8. Your choices have yet to be generated.

9. A broken watch signals a new epoch.

10. It makes no difference where those painted hands point.

11. To keep walking is less a decision than a premonition.

12. The ones who do not answer might just be taking their time, or a polite 'no' may be infinitely better than nothing.

13. You aren't the only one entitled to blight. Complete custody of one toothbrush.

14. The characters *are* 'the city.'

15. He's so hateful yet you wait for his books.

16. I married a funny way of saying it.

17. He's very good at 'the moment.'

18. What I mean is he's adept at being in the moment, not that he's only good at this moment.

19. Should there be an opportunity for you to view the arcane counterfeit we will be sure to let you know.

20. Certain things were not as I imagined.

21. Nakedness, for instance.

22. Actual pictures received by the eye eventually replaced my earnest falsehoods.

23. Bare contagion, beloved.

24. Footsteps pardoned by glitter.

25. Early morning green is every apology.

26. When light moves over each possibility—we wake.

## 03.08.16

1. I admired the sod-filled days.

2. How is your delicate monster, by the way?

3. I want to go back to my pre-screen life.

4. Keeping tasks in mind not open in windows.

5. If I mail myself in pieces will you assemble me when I arrive?

6. Please send soft syllables to counteract harsh edges.

7. The myriad of mind-dissolving missives.

8. Can you save me from those simple requests which extract all initiative?

9. Cross out the ALL CAPS directives, costs we cannot possibly meet.

10. Impossibly illegible stories.

11. Disallow sleep.

12. Beyond sleep of determination.

13. The functionality of rest has been put to bed.

14. A crowd of displacement carries us.

15. A few words slipped into your hand disappeared.

16. Teach me how to prevent words from entering the bloodstream directly through skin.

17. Your descriptions are at risk.

18. When love poems become elegies.

19. I had to partition myself from news.

20. Everything was canceled and I was overjoyed.

21. Don't regret the poorly written line, translate.

22. I had to stay away from your words.

23. How to thin the masses of messages without being depleted?

24. Like walking through a sea of hostile bodies.

25. I wrote to the city, as a visitor.

26. You can't help admiring his slovenly ways.

27. Everything was a disappointment except my ability to help others.

28. My plans were only thoughts.

29. My thoughts were infestations.

30. My itinerary turned to dust.

31. I smiled at the empty sun.

32. My face was pale but you would not mistake me for bloodless.

33. I'm not the only one glad to be alive.

34. Even six neurons, this little worm.

35. Pacify her with documents, modify her with Auntie birds.

1. Bonnie "Prince" Billy sings: I will be born.

2. Is he talking about himself?

3. Is there a difference—

4. Between being one person or another?

5. Waking without remembering dreams is like waking without hands.

6. How to complete any simple action?

7. I cleared my desk of the prints of former cups.

8. Should I have read those markings before wiping them away, first with damp rag, then with dry cloth?

9. I've strayed from divination because I'm not willing to know.

10. When you first recorded what you needed to hear you lived in a single cell.

11. Later you learned to divide.

12. Not yourself but those multiple beings beside you came to life.

13. Meaning to say you decided to see them.

14. And what if you only think you have no hands?

15. Yesterday I asked a fox to appear.

16. This morning a mottled fox dutifully trotted through breakfast.

17. Red and grey, deliberate and languid, delicate and revenant.

18. Maybe you only think you don't see foxes.

19. Or ask for visitation in place of divination.

20. This morning I asked, where are you? Are you still near the other side of cognition?

21. Does deciding to ask for visitations draw you closer, or is that only the fox?

22. Nothing is only. Only is furred.

23. I thought I woke with nothing but I woke with you beside me.

24. I thought I woke, but you were still a promise to remember.

· 25. If there is nothing to fear, why is nothing running? Why does quiet surround me?

26. Quietness is one of the avenues.

27. Nothing is one bright resource.

28. The torch trailing behind you: a deliberate beacon.

## 03.10.16

1. This is a research-based document.

2. My body.

3. Morning migraines may steal dauntlessness.

4. Often avoidable if you know how pacifism is tied up for easy handling.

5. You're still processing yesterday's stray.

6. A twitching eye is related to stratocumulus.

7. Mistaking brightness for sound.

8. He said, I think I am forgetting a certain undetermined or unspecified thing.

9. A string or lace for fastening a shoal.

10. Colder inside the house than outside your shoes.

11. I want to believe certain lines are worthy of wood, thin sheets, wrapping.

12. Does recovery make writing less interesting?

13. What took me one year took you less than an hour.

14. When painkillers don't work turn to your grandmother's china.

15. Drinking infusions in ancestral vessels assists the power of herbal allies.

16. Your head was a rose. Your head was a fisted contagion.

17. My apothecary is underground, beneath skin.

18. When you came home I gave you two choices to alleviate my malady.

19. Making the call is an admission.

20. When you walked in I was dancing loudly.

21. Undressing without a sound.

22. Not physically, nor by choice, not by your own volition.

23. He found himself on paper.

24. Nights being long voiceprints to mend.

25. Either too busy to think or too empty to quench.

26. I placed your poem where it can see out the window.

27. I put myself to bed with a volume of oscillations.

28. Alabaster ledger, thick as cretaceous, collecting appetites for bracken.

29. Alarming numbers fly across the newspaper-covered dawn.

30. I have to remind myself I have been invited to reside inside the infinite.

## 03.11.16

1. Watching steam rise from my cup was an answer.

2. Unfurling sinuous hands, beckoning.

3. Finding you in fields, meadows, roadsides.

4. You were covered in golden scarabs.

5. Yellow blossoms bled to crimson.

6. On the day of longest light.

7. My birth.

8. Becoming an un-disciple, a door opens.

9. Threadbare lists for warmth.

10. Woke determinedly in past-tense deserts.

11. Vehement birds, pink stones, fabled sky.

12. We lifted perishable colors, tasting varieties of light.

13. Letters in place of entire words made me cry.

14. A wooden door flutters like wings.

15. My temperature waves and bends.

16. I miss your tired face nodding through breakfast.

17. Looking down, not speaking, avoiding my gaze.

18. Might we choose to die of exuberance?

19. Do you play the pheromonal theremin?

20. What distinguishes this pose from any other?

21. Absolutely nothing.

# 03.12.16

1. In awe of books not yet arrived, not yet written.

2. What do my shelves say now, every book in unison?

3. Can you hear them?

4. I search for your letter as dusk comes to hide every word.

5. To be a mother is to separate 'm' from myself.

6. Mother becoming 'other.'

7. The other is the child who becomes an adult.

8. Both the parent who lives in childhood and the child whose life is his own.

9. The day was older than it should be.

10. Epigraphs kept shoulders warm.

11. A word for weave and swerve: "werve."

12. They wanted to put an end to the extra hour but it was too expensive.

13. Cannons woke everyone early, to save candles.

14. If a woman behaved that way her statues would look different.

15. Or was the day too young?

16. "But I was so much older then. I'm younger than that now."

17. This concert would not have been possible without decorative mothers escorting flocks.

18. I saw the distance between where he sat and where he intended to rise.

19. When the music began I understood his ambivalence perfectly.

20. This was only one possible path, one chair in a symphony, one vibrating note.

21. Please refer to all the useful things she does: telepathic shoes.

22. Gladly did I part with every letter of my name.

23. Through your unwavering support we find plural homes.

24. Tier by tier. Person by glove.

25. One character leans against another.

26. In certain light we are indiscernible.

# 03.13.16

1. Why do I resist the obvious?

2. I never use that entrance, as if it doesn't exist.

3. Start paying attention to the details of your life.

4. So I need not remember them.

5. He embarked upon that treacherous passage toward his second youth.

6. His first adulthood.

7. The notion that the day is an open doorway, a counter to sit at, inscribing.

8. As if the enclosed hours did not echo, did not contain strings.

9. Keep walking by your own refusals, releasing all circuits.

10. Did you choose to be the author of your fears?

11. All along I knew I wasn't here. I had to stop dreaming you. But didn't.

12. I loved several sources I did not know. They did not protect me from myself.

13. Collecting languages I did not speak.

14. Bodies I could not enter.

15. Voices whose charm resided in remoteness.

16. Why is distance a compelling opiate?

17. I speak as if I knew where I were, where you are, where we are all to be.

18. I started timing my discomfort.

19. Later I looked at the numbers and found them infinitely smaller than promised.

20. Why isn't it enough for me to love your trauma?

21. Why must I love the trauma of the unknown?

22. All I ask is that you maintain the facade.

23. Chewing glass, holding your breath, petting alligators.

24. Please let me leave you alone.

25. To be the reader of your own fears.

26. She thanked me for relieving her of carrying a key.

27. Our plot was based on a story—which archive, which noir?

# 03.14.16

1. These words exist to be your friends.

2. Placating every feather.

3. In the unwalking rain.

4. You could say the garment cascades down her sides.

5. But how many sides have you seen?

6. A captive feminism so variable the weave rearranges itself each minute.

7. Another sequestered self.

8. Once dressed she danced in any weather.

9. A word I have looked up over and over and don't understand any better.

10. I reread the handwritten letter on lavender paper then ripped it to shreds.

11. The floor became visible for the first time in months.

12. Arriving home from various travels we place our minds here and there in canvas bags.

13. Trying to type while holding open a dictionary with both hands.

14. As if either side of the book were the back of a bird.

15. An efficient console, loading the base of palms with content.

16. Do we really exist in program notes, train tickets, and postcards?

17. No coincidence in coming to the end of a handwritten journal as one book expires and another begins.

18. You carry the remnants of trees on your lap. Firs, flat and fragrant, crown knees.

19. One line of light bisects each needle.

20. When agitation rose beyond reason you entered the chamber hung low and verdant.

21. Your voice alone bristled.

22. Walking, page turning, opening cupboards and drawers.

23. You consumed all available air, leaving me tarnished, incomparable.

24. Not fit for any civilized compass.

25. I stalked cameos, those iridescent replicas of women.

26. Or merely their glimmering blue profiles.

27. The last time we lived inside drawings with nothing in common, rooms with pulled shades—

28. We must learn to be separate persons.

29. After decades we still sometimes forget.

30. Falsely idealized marrow.

31. My demise was reverentially planned.

32. I underlined the selves later to be replaced.

33. We do not stop when arms grow tired.

34. I exist to be your friend.

1. Days when everything must be done later.

2. That school of "not now."

3. When the date alarms you, interchange numbers.

4. March 75, 6021.

5. A fine year to misunderstand.

6. When frightened about elections I try to recall many things eventually sync.

7. Translations for the reading that never happened.

8. You recommend a book whose main character invites me to dinner.

9. I would have had no idea my host was a fiction.

10. Asked to rewrite the inappropriate lyric, then to sing it onstage.

11. You fall asleep in all the wrong places.

12. Irises and hyacinths are uncertain when to raise their heads.

13. Every storm performs the work of adamant sculptors.

14. The ground is adorned with mottled limbs, tulip tree libations.

15. I print out the list of recurring associations, wondering what I've missed.

16. Read about the exile of phenomenal units of sound.

17. Write letters of invitation to words I cannot pronounce.

18. She wrote: I have doubts about my ability to coordinate eventuality.

19. Euphoria wore a minuscule green coterie, a countenance drenched.

20. These next few items can only be referred to as: Sisyphus, motion sickness, and the land of one's ancestors.

21. If only naming fecundity could endow me with cover, coven.

# 03.16.16

1. I scrolled between two messages, one from incapacity, the other from radiance.

2. You'd think my choice would be easy, yet I answer to both.

3. I walked forward in the problematic garment and the security guards asked me to disrobe.

4. I placed metallic understanding under the scrutiny of powerful cameras.

5. Yet walked through the passage virtually unchanged.

6. Decrepit faucets were leeching lead, toxic speech under the guise of policy.

7. The edges of dreams retreated, an ocean repeating the letter "c."

8. In the middle of the night I was surprised by what I was ambivalent to remember.

9. So this is where my unconscious has gathered.

10. Fixed upon remains of light-sensitive crystals.

11. Cellulose and silver resolution escaped me.

12. I read the message one last time before turning on the radio news.

13. The idea was to retrieve something which would protect me.

14. A process I could only approach in silence.

15. Before the clamor of my wide-eyed kitchen.

16. Earliness is an asset and sleepiness may sometimes be ignored.

17. Eggs, scones, tea, and fresh fruit before school.

18. Younger kids should start earlier and teenagers should sleep in.

19. I want to read every one of your books.

20. Why would I ever stop befriending words?

21. I am going to that country where death isn't real.

22. Because the object of my obsession remained unmet it was easily replicable.

23. I've only been to your language as a tourist.

24. Because the reminder note on the counter was no longer necessary I became attached.

25. I considered taking the poor drawing into a shop and asking.

26. The wave of relief was so palpable all flesh released from bones.

27. Like sitting at a counter writing by hand.

28. Never abandoned by thought.

29. I'm just beginning.

30. My reading was a map to every love.

31. Love was a map to every delicacy, every sorrow.

32. The entrance is on the same level as the sidewalk.

33. I was taken back, in few words, to a time we understood each other.

34. Why is it so easy to be dead wrong about our own personal histories?

35. They spent their talents at the spiel.

36. I wrote his name on the heel of my shoe to make it disappear.

1. I couldn't bear to go out in the non-committal fog.

2. To meet reliably throbbing companions.

3. Remembering the empty dress beside you I leapt up.

4. What are you having for dinner?

5. *V v v v v—little beasties,* you said.

6. Nothing I can imagine will impede the pale plummeting of time.

7. Sound of metal spoon against ceramic vessel.

8. Do I want the experience or do I just want to be home and have it be already over?

9. She wrote: *Nothing is more important than Barcelona or just getting out there.*

10. Too much happening at once is never blank, the perfect blindness.

11. Like watching the young mother who has no time to consider death.

12. She signed up to have a baby, then a toddler then a child, nothing taller.

13. Adolescence is something that happens to other people's kids.

14. She assumes her parents will never die, and 'later' is still a bounteous category.

15. I can only speak for myself.

16. Regardless of the facts of loss, dissolution, and factioning.

17. Later is narrow or non-existent. I'm finally convinced.

18. Don't blame the young mother and don't envy her either.

19. At nightfall, don't watch videos of your kids in their pajamas trying to assemble their first musical instruments.

20. Especially after signing them up for SATs.

21. Cancel disease. Cancel doors. Cancel distance. Allow distance.

22. They will mistake you. They will ask why.

23. Because you cannot commandeer. Because care is close to carry.

24. Because in some dictionaries 'communicate' is near 'communion.'

25. Wait. Because the number of births at any given time, because you are warm-blooded.

26. Arrange your forelimbs into modified wings.

27. Take them on trips. Feed them. Ask them what they think. Insist on embracing.

28. Embrace bafflement.

29. Tell them only what they can possibly hear and make use of in the moment.

30. To the friend who asks a question about boundary-seeking, say the same thing.

31. A teacher told me when I was very young that my greatest fault was my age.

32. Try not to waste breath.

33. Call me as many names as you like. I'm collecting.

34. Names, trying them on.

35. Dear creature of the notebook.

36. Reach out your spindly arms.

37. Home is the center of the unknown beast.

38. Delinquent and in search of language.

39. I'm sorry I could not stop the dredging of your mind.

40. I attempted to disallow time and failed.

41. Still with you amid anxiety I am powerless to assuage.

42. Sometimes I sing to you on the phone.

43. Any song with the word "sunshine."

44. Looking back was an anchor—or looking back we drown.

# 03.18.16.1

1. How often do you want what you've forgotten you already possess?

2. I read her journal entries as if I had written them myself.

3. The red box lined in satin had no characters I could read.

4. A project list with hieroglyphic manners.

5. Freshly painted tea leaves, geometric-therapy.

6. Dates of service: rain, mud, seraphic games.

7. Haven't I learned anything?

8. Because I sent you my eggs and arranged your nest I think I am entitled to plumage.

9. If I didn't know better I'd call myself imperceptible.

10. Why go in search of neglect?

11. Determined to repeat the same failings with each person.

12. Partners in grime.

13. Two out of three and you pine for the third.

14. Don't you know all thirds are careless?

15. How do I interpret what has not yet occurred?

## 03.18.16.2

1. Your exit is above your head.

2. Move the handle in the direction of the red arrow.

3. Slides detach to form rafts fitted with lights and whistles.

4. Pull the mask toward your second face.

5. Awaiting a message which did not arrive I was more than tempted to write it myself.

6. But where do these observations belong?

7. "As if certain notes written in my diary up to now had merely been rough drafts of my own life" (Enrique Vila-Matas).

8. The difference between the written and the lived collapses nicely, a fan, the blink of a life, the edge of a cliff.

9. The absence of breath.

10. Either I walk blindly through the airport or we pause to open my suitcase.

11. "Truly, what we call the 'novel' is nothing more than this ongoing conversation" (Enrique Vila-Matas).

12. Between life and literature.

13. To travel with (or as) a real person, as opposed to an apparition, does present inconveniences.

14. But the opposite is also true.

15. In flight all systems of measurement disappeared including age and location.

16. His mistake was not in assuming that this singular task was reliant upon another person, but that each endeavor is also sealed in simultaneity.

17. So what allows us to continue?

18. He erroneously thought his actions were his own.

19. Was I going mad or did everyone suddenly resemble you?

20. The man studying is you with a slightly more weathered book.

21. And that voice I never heard must have been yours, though in another body.

22. And that walk was reminiscent of the way you sit in a chair.

23. Since when did it become only the remarks that are not made which are most important?

24. Reading the novel was another way of being with you.

25. Your presence was so insistent you almost began to exist.

26. In the same way a teacher once called out to me in a crowded room, "your thought was loud!"

27. The words exited her mouth in the same way one follows the next.

28. In the way a man with his head turned away from me, looking out a window, so I can't see his face, could be you.

29. Who did I think I was—entering the unknown so deliberately?

30. But is it any safer to do so unintentionally?

31. Home is now many words away, and many steps and hours.

32. Why do I allow almost every narrative to deteriorate?

33. Am I trying to be true to life or to deny the narratives I cannot accept?

34. Unable to dream a way out.

35. Paying attention does not guarantee adaptation.

36. Yet is distractedness any better?

37. The action of writing began to smooth out unruly thoughts.

38. Until I could almost run my hands all the way through, in one continuous motion, without resistance.

39. Small snags in theory; slow movements in sand.

40. I combed the darkness hoping it contained stars.

1. Hurray for the friendship of our words!
2. We are actually going to be where we said we were.
3. He abandoned the book wherever he was when finished.
4. Did you feel affection for handwriting?
5. I could not see curves any more than I could see my own body.
6. Like a vehicle in which one moves forward.
7. Leaving us free to draw around ourselves an inscrutable carriage.
8. My disbelief was equal only to my anticipation.
9. Soon I would enter an alphabet of streets, bridges and buildings.
10. Old stone is not only a way to speak but a mind to inhabit.
11. I made my face into yours as I slept.
12. In dreams a new setting approached.
13. The last word pronounces itself as we arrive.

# 03.21.16

1. I thanked her pseudonym.

2. Over dinner we were told, while in the local area we must eat hand-harvested sentences.

3. We were also advised that such sentences were too expensive, so we should avoid them.

4. Perhaps instead we could buy and cook our own text from the open market. Perhaps instead we would eat shelled words.

5. We were told about the dangers of harvesting round alphabets (persons drown peril).

6. They said we could witness halos of prose, soft bodies hurled across rocks.

7. Flesh softened so as to make it more palatable.

8. Perhaps it is unethical to harvest small aesthetically divine circles of prose.

9. Edges illegible.

10. But wasn't diminishing visibility your ultimate purpose?

11. Or was invisibility just a circumstance of persistence?

12. She handed me the copies of the original handwritten manuscript saying *you have not seen this*.

13. In other words, I can admit I have seen a document I am not permitted to name.

14. But isn't one always permitted to pronounce symbols in place of the unnameable?

15. Aren't you more interested in a text not yet available?

16. Connectivity in the air as ocean, or in translation of water to air.

17. A walk toward an unseen though tangible presence.

18. We had no idea of the time, and talked on.

19. Her forceful proclamations vibrating.

20. Do not draw a box around my words.

21. How will the next generations describe themselves?

22. Is brevity the ultimate excuse?

23. I wondered how long it would take before a certain name plummeted into the room, how long before the name would stampede across the table.

24. We could avoid names for only so long.

25. Public space is, in itself, the desired city in any language.

26. Language of footsteps in public gardens.

27. Sounds of fortresses in tears.

28. Walk with me along the promontory.

29. I wonder how you pay at these faces.

30. She kept saying 'and then I asked' without revealing her question.

31. A story woven entirely of digression.

32. Whose turn is it to ruin this street?

33. An unfinished series of diagrams.

34. It was impossible to tell what the clouds awaited.

35. Shadows fell from hulls, glossy and whispering.

## 03.22.16

1. These smudges used to be animals.

2. All horned heads aligned.

3. Robes, archways, levitation.

4. Honeycomb on the undersides of detached mural painting.

5. Yellow clouds, edges adorned with hindsight.

6. Bordered blue an oblong blankness.

7. Angling up in curved lines.

8. Wings flocked in eyes.

9. Placed in a cauldron.

10. I set out to photograph amulet traces, to make a visual corollary.

11. But how to photograph bone through all of those clothes?

12. How to make a ghost stand still?

13. Endless preparations to approach an eight-eyed beast.

14. What is the meaning of droves of eyes?

15. There he is again, dutifully on his cross.

16. Decorative globular fringes hang from his beard.

17. Hold out your hands; paint them with mead.

18. Dear wise woman inscribed in cupola.

19. A lamb adorns your pale crown.

20. Meet me at the cradle of never-ending dawn.

21. Pull down that straying sheep by the high window.

22. Don't you know detached heads placed upon scales are already tame?

23. Dragons atop curling waves send arrows back upon archers.

24. Birds with metal chambers hidden in their backs await missives.

25. Reliquaries embossed with stars.

26. Fall into this miniature crimson ocean.

27. A castle hung on a hook.

28. The queen holds a pink minaret in one hand.

29. Fleece, asleep on a book.

30. A woman kneels on heaps of flames.

31. Could painting her portrait save her?

32. White fading to white.

33. I find this room terrifying.

34. Though it all happened centuries ago.

35. Tying the snouts of crocodiles closed with rags.

## 03.25.16

1. What to wear with ruffled sky.
2. A blue Parisian pale silk song.
3. That's fine work finding new ice cream.
4. Wasting time in the written city.
5. Busily sewing an "I."
6. Replacing a zipper.
7. Almost missed the importance of a woman with a needle.
8. A visitation.
9. But can this really be mended?
10. How surprised we were thinking only one past must be exchanged for a future.
11. We sat in silent stitchery.
12. Every moment at first impatient.
13. Later I saw urgency.
14. Sewn together.
15. And then pleasure, along scars.
16. Whole and entire.

# 03.26.16

1. Now that I am home who will extinguish marrow?
2. One rhythm was broken, another stranded.
3. A third waited, a chain around my neck.
4. Becoming someone older than fiction.
5. Nice trick, or mess, or wreck.
6. I asked myself to meet me.
7. But I was very aloof.
8. Or not at home to the idea of knowing how.
9. Little suffragettes were washing windows.
10. But the other side of the glass looked out onto nothing.
11. A problem of framing.
12. Sorry to waste good soap and rags.
13. Even sadder when human efforts fail.
14. How to ignore druthers while also throwing away spare idiocy.
15. How to walk toward new foundations.
16. Hillsides made of light.
17. Skin erupted in crimson sanctions.
18. Addiction to repetitions.
19. It's nice to be in bed with an open book.
20. Or to be an open book.
21. Transposed into a window.
22. The book illuminates the room.
23. I read you between coverings.
24. You only exaggerate when you close your eyes.

## 03.27.16

1. A necessary affront, a first sentence.
2. Time taken to write by hand.
3. Allows thoughts which occur between.
4. Hidden music.
5. Recurrences as signals, ligatures.
6. A potent dose of imaginary life.
7. That connection between dose and does.
8. Morning a milky white window with composition of dark branches.
9. Echoed like one long elusive dedication.
10. A text that could not be written, only whispered.
11. As we woke, were we now returned?
12. Where does all elapsed accumulate?
13. Behind eyes, mirrors of hands?
14. We are images yet to be language.
15. A careless collage of selves.

# 03.28.16

1. I won't drink the published version of our meeting.

2. Sublime subjects.

3. Events in little red book.

4. I'm solely sunk.

5. A gallery of no substance, no content.

6. Yet every glimmering absence remains.

7. The idea was to become less an obstacle.

8. Concepts kept me from realism.

9. Malleable thought, confiscated hands.

10. Presence is the nearness of breath.

11. Crystallized light.

12. I described a lack of manageable alphabets as follows:

13. Why subsist on letters?

14. How well can you think any else's thoughts?

*Words have their own minds.*

1. You are the beneficiary of my culinary impulses.

2. Please don't be over me.

3. No number of pages will be enough, and yet the book has to end somewhere.

4. Rejection of closure marries rejection of finishing a book.

5. The correct title for the manuscript is the one the author chooses.

6. Is that opening apparatus too assuming to be burdened by emptiness?

7. Your first place frightens me.

8. Superstitions are purloined but the arrangement is mine.

9. How often do you hide from your art?

10. Even this pile of newspapers is suspect.

11. She said the title would light up in gold letters, but it has not happened yet.

12. I'm not her, and she is not me, you are not they and I am not we.

13. Still we get along pretty well, they say.

14. I only love in plural, too risky to pick just one.

15. Besides identity is a construct molded by many.

16. Shall we talk about what goes on or stay inside affliction?

17. How to ask not a person, but a myth?

18. Tell me about your life as an escort to the city.

19. Anything I write about X is problematic.

20. Considering my almost human beginnings.

## 04.08.16

1. The light blew through my words but a shadow of my hand remained.

2. Fine to be a chronicler of social ills, but can you live on that?

3. I got myself up, exercised, fed, clean and set, and then I went to harvest something to counteract drudgery, cynicism and even fate.

4. I write against the hopeless moment, the one when we realize how little difference our efforts make.

5. I wrote against your body, my favorite pressure.

6. I write because you wrote and in your words we all had words.

7. Inside the word 'inside' is shelter.

8. Come inside.

## 04.10.16

1. Your problem with time isn't unbearable, but that you have no fitting false starts.

2. Is something really wrong or is that just error smiling?

3. When will we be alright?

4. Hard to remember that he is not me.

5. When no one shows up you eat alone.

6. When powerless, I write.

7. What kind of message was I expecting to save me?

8. Implausible, but true, an inbox radiates love.

9. You line up your "selves" and ask them to talk.

10. What if they (you) don't trust you?

11. We arrive in a house not yet unpacked.

12. We live among boxes containing childhoods forgotten.

13. A pair of too pale jeans, zip at the ankles.

14. You try lives on to see what fits.

15. But it wasn't my house and we are talking to the dead.

16. A poet who planned to retire in a mythical state constructed solely of sun.

17. We are so happy for you, we say, of her new digs.

18. But mostly we're just glad to see her—again—alive.

## 04.11.16

1. If I pull you toward me will I remember?

2. Violets survived snows.

3. Grow back thickly, green skies.

4. I aspire to emulate your generous admonition.

5. If only I could, decade by decade, weave myself more densely into the hush.

6. Kiss every triumphant leaf.

7. I ignored the signs of my body dissolving.

8. If I pull you nearer, will you talk, humble half-full notebook?

9. The one to drive must admit where we are going.

10. Afraid, designed, ashamed.

11. Words have their own minds.

12. Come on, let's go.

13. While wakefully handling the details of one parent's sad decline I make final edits to the death of the other.

14. In my sleep I visit their able-bodied futures and camp out in the not yet unpacked houses of dead poets I love.

15. The dangers of one sadness effacing another, or the confusion of subtle veins opening endlessly.

16. They all lead to the same knot, the same series of vestibules, windows revealing birds beating against glass.

17. What else should I ignore as I draw your face closer, if only on paper?

18. Why won't you recognize yourself in these drawings?

19. Please don't disown your earlier selves.

20. For one thing, they won't give up.

21. When did inclusivity become lonely?

22. Empathy was more than a kitchen chair, less than a stovepipe.

23. You gave birth to several mesmerizing haunts.

24. Lamented the death of a lamppost, a gathering spot for moths.

25. Tried to cover your voice as if you could keep the previous one as a souvenir.

26. Every one of you is still interior to the school of noise.

27. My third parent was unable to walk.

28. How many do you have?

29. To be given life is also to laugh.

# 04.12.16.1

1. In the fourteenth month in the year of somnambulism.

2. Everything must be done twice for no reason.

3. Update your evolutionary tree.

4. Look up at the new moon after buying envelopes.

5. All 'laters' default, are befallen to 'now.'

6. And then the dread of something non-existent, such as a future absence.

7. Humans, flowers, amoebas all on a slender twig.

8. Hulking, almost legible, about to erupt.

9. Meadowsoil.

10. You followed me all the way home.

11. We got our start as simple life-forms.

12. You being sacrosanct yet indistinct.

13. Dominated by species scientists have never seen.

14. To leave the house before writing is (a) often (b) necessary.

15. If only (never) were an option.

16. Like going naked on the subway.

17. Try to stop imagining how little we might accomplish.

18. If we'd succumbed to candid and chilly mortality.

19. An agonized confession.

20. Eligible for countless progeny.

21. Why so elusive, all those iterations?

22. Architectures tugging sleeves.

23. I turn on the light to avoid one blindness.

24. An unseen terror kept me company.

25. Who offered permissions to lie down, not yet dressed, to write and to look out a window?

26. Rain on trees does not subscribe to non-rhythmic incumbents.

27. Taking apart bewildered worlds.

# 04.12.16.2

1. Remember to protect yourself from the power of words.
2. Introvert much?
3. Homely reciprocity hinders homesickness.
4. Thwarts familiar alienation.
5. Ground mocks social gaps.
6. Nothing is not one thing.
7. Face to irreparable face.
8. Agamben can't write solid fog.
9. Losing one's way is an advantageous prologue.
10. Marginal, tragic, fabled, bent.
11. So much to read *is* action.
12. Transition is a walk, block by block.
13. Unbirth.
14. Brow transmission.
15. The background is bones.
16. All we've read along the way.

## 04.14.16

1. Every morning small children watch you race to the bus stop amazed at your speed, cheering you on.

2. Her voice wasn't the uppity victim you'd supposed.

3. More like a semi-hysterical blister.

4. You awake to the letter 'N.'

5. Disappointing as your pen running out.

6. Even if I comfort myself with dregs.

7. Misinformation is a gullible curtain.

8. Can you hear me?

9. I'm talking to that specialized concentration I hope will show up.

10. Difference, a great dane up a tree.

11. A rescue harness, a tarp.

12. I don't want to be the seventy-four-year-old woman lost in the desert for nine days.

13. Nor do I wish to be your dog.

14. I enjoyed the evening with nincompoops more than the night of high fevers.

15. Please remember to continue signing as yourself.

16. I used to be able to hide from myself in the perfect dress.

17. But love in the time of spectacle only caters to formfitting flare.

18. Am I blue to understand you or because of the emptiness of color?

19. Which fading is most unbearable at dusk?

20. Does completing your elegy suggest I finally believe you aren't here?

21. My icon said no.

22. Now I know how diffusion makes effrontery kindred.

23. Why didn't I cultivate more of those less ramshackled composites?

24. Tell no one my instincts and bury my crimes.

## 04.15.16

1. Would it be presumptuous if I were to give her a name?

2. I don't hesitate to affectionately place titles at the top of every stage.

3. We go through.

4. Countless scenes in which I am your granddaughter.

5. Today you would have been one hundred and four.

6. And this other absence.

7. I'll call her Violet.

8. Triumphant and numerous, smiling up at me from the lawn.

9. Startlingly awake.

10. Impossible to write the word impossible.

11. Instead I will write "how."

12. To love our broken paucity.

13. My idea of perfect beforehands isn't even worth rewrapping.

14. Still, I bother to transpose myself.

15. It's part of your private profile to see my faithful sidereal.

16. Transmissions prearranged.

17. By passing stars.

18. Can you see a lily planting constellations?

19. Her hand looks exactly like mine.

20. What do I do to be that person?

21. Forward flight forward flight forward—

22. A careful solitary friction.

23. Call me when you love it.

24. Leaves, I like your thinking.

25. To write through an entire life: *nothing* being always fantastic.

26. Having read the entire alphabet, once, twice.

27. Mess with it.

28. Off with my head, clear my desk (dis)ease, become other.

29. Afraid of prying lists. What have I done?

30. The number of numbers kept us wet and cold.

31. Subsisting on syntactical nimbus.

32. You wanted her ring and I was happy for you to have it.

33. I'm so glad she left me her hands.

## 04.17.16.1

1. A length of cloth falls
2. Over me like water
3. Form is never static
4. Folds and drapes are motions constructing meaning
5. Craving the swish of skirts
6. Her unstated perfume evaporated and all depth was gone
7. Those arms so lovely
8. But it was not furnishings nor dimensions nor location or light
9. Not the promise of a room in a flutter of garments
10. What animates
11. If I place pen to paper will I find out
12. Gold lettering disappears, margins
13. Numbers to the left vanish
14. Yet all remain as remnants to remind
15. Each line is finite and fallible

1. I stayed up later than my body
2. Determined and strange
3. Am I less cynical unbroken
4. Unpaid labor frowns
5. Invisible, redundant with womanhood
6. So many of my pages part to places I'd rather not say
7. As I write this curled in sheets on my side
8. Like a vestigial comma
9. Knees bent to a V
10. Base of spine, sacred basin
11. In a line from sacrum to skull
12. Am I a less broken division of labor
13. Biology was on my side
14. I married biology and gave birth
15. To write as a mother created matter
16. My children learned to speak, multiplying my efforts
17. A rope was put around my neck but I was not broken
18. My back was vertical
19. I carried only those I chose

1. How to live with (our)selves now—first blankness.

2. Beyond birds attacking their own reflections.

3. The list of things to do does not lean in.

4. I'm a telepathic activist doing laundry, rearranging bones.

5. After the unbearable crescendo I went outside to pick up sticks.

6. She said the ghost had been with her since birth.

7. I said my mother was my other and my fiction was a daughter.

8. The sun shone on the weeds, on the adolescent leaves.

9. On the ivy climbing a tree.

10. The sun was everywhere except inside his idea of himself.

11. The sunlight in his body ate holes in that interior garment he did not believe.

12. But what about the light the body cannot perceive?

13. Fear is enough to distort even this pristine spring into an unrepeatable utterance.

14. He required a very powerful avatar to blot out his brilliance.

15. You don't need to search far to consume suffering.

16. How else can I stare into a distance that does not exist?

17. Close your eyes and we are all made of darkness.

18. Or not.

19. But what lives inside.

20. We say this happens to others.

21. Yet we are all.

22. Others.

23. The ruin of the poet is not the ruling of the reader.

## 04.20.16

1. When required to speak frankly about something we wish did not exist.

2. I enter the room to search though don't know what I'm searching for.

3. You can keep the words crossed out but you cannot hurt yourself.

4. When the next line doesn't come I squint.

5. Remember music escorts you.

6. Follows your every tortured step.

7. You don't believe me?

8. I have to imagine you are being followed.

9. By benevolence.

10. Some impulses are impossible to abbreviate.

11. For instance, at that point I could have talked for ten hours and still would have remained unsatiated, provoked.

12. Broken is as broken as the myriad shards you shelter.

13. Every one of them an eye.

14. Not only that but a similar ritual or routine is occurring on every corner.

15. In every basement or forest.

16. Any place humans exist.

17. You want to see yourself as a particularity.

18. One day you won't be sorry you aren't.

19. And are.

20. What you are beyond thoughts is not to be denied.

21. We'll still have plenty of violets.

22. Promise me.

1. I'll tell you when you get to fall apart.
2. She said to herself.
3. Not now.
4. The month was running away with itself.
5. Nothing I could do.
6. Actually your list has never been longer.
7. Which means you have a strange way of populating nothing.
8. The ten thousand flowering objects.
9. Mouths, timetables, ingredients.
10. Waiting is most difficult when one is—waiting.
11. Weight and wade and wide.
12. When is it safe to wrap you in a blanket and allow you to dream?
13. She recreated me over the phone.
14. Then told me how long to immerse, pluck, mix and braise.
15. What would you fold into these leaves?
16. Secure packages with paint and psalms with science.
17. Your paper letter arrived, reminding me of our new name.
18. Insects wrote books.
19. Now I know: I'm you, me, and everyone.
20. You have already survived your darkest power.

1. You were inside me so I couldn't see you.

2. I cried however many suns I was allowed.

3. Until my eyes irradiant.

4. Pronounced an even meter of loss.

5. That a car can take you somewhere.

6. I can't live here.

7. Sorry.

8. I don't care how far.

9. We might have to unravel.

10. The faces of my children at every age look out at me.

11. Without you I don't exist.

12. I enter a room and your photograph is present.

13. Can I recognize a time before portraits were problematic?

14. Because time isn't beside us, but the river.

15. Inside your visceral light.

16. Departs sidelines.

17. I don't stop because I find no end.

## 04.23.16

1. Your newly born human is an entire woman.
2. A stunning mimesis.
3. A self-closing study in sinuous form.
4. A visual alphabet.
5. Asleep on matte snow.
6. Words themselves perform folding.
7. Triggers, harmoniums, translations.
8. Migrating thought is like five-dimensional weather.
9. We are surrounded by winter.
10. Construction of art does not mean we mustn't.
11. Superimpose, compose or erase—interiors.
12. Sublime stone, sullen or moss covered.
13. Emblems—fetal curls at base.
14. Snowborn delirium—references bending.
15. One medium into another.
16. Bodies coil, days end, light returns.
17. Sheaths of skin form canopies, skies.
18. A few lines escape, hover.
19. You look out into silver.
20. Speaking silences stop then start again.
21. Precipitously propel green to emerge.
22. Barrenness to reveal.

23. What mattered less—was matter.

24. What matters more is the way you describe yourself.

25. When you were alone you were always—

26. With one of your speaking silences.

27. But which one?

# 04.24.16

1. A mottled fox trotted through carding
2. Grateful to see you—I took it as a sign
3. Spinning loped to one perimeter, posed at edging
4. Under the dogwood—pale cups opening
5. Another version of song
6. Without any sound
7. Skies, setting adverbs
8. Please
9. Don't disappear

# 04.25.16.1

1. Lull of the hand
2. Passed along matrilineal lines
3. Shaken not buried
4. Steadies thought against a keen edge
5. Breath between each line
6. Encourages all you never wrought
7. Possible
8. And yet the word 'thought' is predominant
9. Overused and burdensome
10. Taken apart we have: ought, out, gut
11. Add 's' to find ghost and gust
12. The only curves are in the 'g'
13. Tug, hut
14. Though tough, 'thought,' thug
15. Only a tot
16. Go

## 04.25.16.2

1. Loneliness was ours
2. I never was, nor ever sat quietly
3. Inside a covered antagonistic wagon
4. Listen shudder
5. Would you rather keep me company walking backward
6. Following lint
7. Floating as if weightedness were the only predicament
8. Would I feel less alone if solitude were mine
9. If only one idea half followed another creating a series of steps
10. A solid walk, a destination
11. Instead I stirred the mixture one second too long
12. A glossy polish turned to sand
13. Sounds of running water mixed with
14. Wordless improvised dallying
15. Over and over she repeated
16. *batshit, broken fences, a leak*
17. Or just a hose left running
18. Boxes in a basement, shedding
19. If anxiety were more forthcoming
20. You might explain things to the ground
21. Only my hand is trained to guide
22. My mind toward even landings

## 04.26.16

1. Don't stop to read yourself

2. Hurry further into words as the only remedy

3. For incurable—lives

4. Rafts of blossoming utterance

5. Secrets whispered to the centers of flowers

6. Petaled cups, fringed in lashes

7. Bodies laced in leaves

8. Here I reside in spring on the first floor, along with trunks

9. Adamant beings who stand upright regardless

10. Inner muck rising, reservations

11. What is turmoil to a solid statement

12. Immovable sutures

13. The way your poem was described in the *NYT*

14. The poet fails tragically to create space for herself free of our global worries

15. As if the aspiration of poetry

16. Were to reside in mock reality wherein we might find

17. Real "fake" comfort in literature

18. As if poetry exists to tell soothing lies

19. Which is the same proof of convulsive chatter

20. Now in the face of you'd-never-guess

21. Pulverized pasts everywhere

22. He said he liked talking to the broken as if they were a subset—
I said

23. Welcome newly awake human—to our myriad broken worlds

# 04.28.16.1

1. Nothing to do about all this affection
2. You whom I have rarely seen
3. Occupy a normative
4. Enormity—
5. Can I really write in any position
6. I'll tell this machine what I can't say to you
7. We try not to remember what destroys us
8. How different I felt when dressed for the day
9. Who is that person sulking
10. Did I admire nothingness too much
11. Along with the incessant speech of writers
12. Every word knew me well
13. But did I personally know any of those words
14. So many said: I've given up verbs
15. Others said they would never again throw their arms around artifice
16. One confided he desired to distrust the actual
17. Another lamented the loneliness of objects
18. But what I really want to say about loneliness—
19. I've decided to keep you
20. And therefore to keep loneliness always beside me
21. Or was it loyalty

22. And will you also always be lonely for those selves

23. We once knew in our others as we single-mindedly move

24. Into age—as if we had a choice

25. Love is that understanding that we will always be lonely

26. For an aspect impossible to close

27. And that other loneliness we call loneliness

28. An unreliable well

29. I've lived inside forgetfulness as a way to avoid my own

30. How can I blame her for her neglect of verbs

31. How could I blame him for refusing to replace

32. Himself in public with the less-neurotic, written self refused

33. How can I blame you for living far away

34. From that actuality we call friendship

35. With absent body and clarifying eyes

## 04.28.16.2

1. I thought I was busy but in truth I'd gone to sleep
2. When asked about that line she said: I was only quoting heroines
3. Why should I speak of my own feelings
4. When those of others are readily available
5. Why need any one person feel exactly as they do
6. As if solitary emotions were possible
7. I wished to write a fourteen-line poem in which
8. Every phoneme was the equivalent of
9. A search for the friend of my art
10. A problematical statement, though true
11. How might one restate this
12. I am entirely serious and just as capable
13. Of imaginary calamity as anyone else
14. We could begin with the question
15. Why is a friend not always beside me
16. And if there is no end to this strange compulsion to write
17. Where to begin; isn't the wish for a friend identical
18. It was of no consolation to her whatsoever
19. That many people behave in a similarly idiotic manner
20. A torrent of words, book after book, beyond control
21. All I can do is transcribe and set
22. Aside words for the day they may find

23. Their place in the hands

24. Of a sympathetic reader

25. You could call a survey of mortality

26. More than an abstract study

27. I miss terribly those who constructed me closely

28. Fastened to poetic audacity: Hannah, Leslie, Stacy, C. D.

29. Still, I want to say to all my words: I don't have time for you

30. My native language, it's nothing

31. Why do I think I am always supposed to like the speaker of a poem

32. Friendship is the opposite of haplessness

33. When I say friendship I mean the opposite of ruin

34. I wish I could forget who I am when I'm writing

35. And sometimes I do but never for long enough

36. It's not that I dislike night but that friction

37. Is relentless and clouds never leave

38. I'm standing here at the sink trying to figure out how to speak

39. Into this little microphone while brushing my teeth

40. Because thoughts offer no rest

41. Time for meditation

42. With the kind of frequency I once took

43. For granted: persons I loved did not die

44. Lakey said: *little kids little problems*

45. Adolescence is a rocket

46. I wish I had one permanently consoling sentence

47. What's happening with frequencies on the page

48. I went to a doctor specifically for writers

49. Who asked—how are things coming along

50. So many ill-starters can't write

51. Deconstructed by overwork they don't have time

52. But I can't stop

53. In a cold room in a paper robe—whoever

54. Thought of that particular torture; I grew

55. Warm, tossed off my gown and strutted

56. I'm normally shy but in this fiction I'm not

57. I said to the doctor: WORDS won't leave me alone

58. Please let me live long enough to care

59. For my endless children and other particular tasks

60. Of the soul. He said: that's the most ridiculous

61. Sentence ever. Do writers have soluble sovereignty

62. Maybe I'd be better off if I covered my hands

63. With paint and then walked on them

64. Practicing inverted postures

65. Does one neurosis mirror another

66. What I want to say to you is endless

67. Sorcery and so this page was born

68. We're always looking for the story that is in our likelihood

69. Especially now and maybe that's why I read Aira

70. He keeps moving ahead as if there were no

71. Almost, as if tomorrow were already here

1. Headfirst I search the dictionary
2. For florescence
3. Dispensation of empress powerdive
4. Did I need to ruin perfectly flung
5. Decaying wood, temporal foolscap
6. Pointed muzzle, erect ears
7. Fur of this social
8. Foyer—frabjous
9. Obscene or scurrilous freight
10. Your former geological age
11. Running through someone other than
12. A continuous supply of pink-ink-
13. I-like-to-drink—melt or pour
14. Into a house founded on solid
15. Drooping tubular purple or white
16. Variegated hours which open
17. Late afternoons
18. Stained yellowish brown
19. Parachutes of an old book

## 04.30.16.2

1. Sorry I didn't call
2. My dreams of you were all I could bear
3. Does it count if I speak to you here
4. I'd like to think the cognizant parts of you
5. Fled somewhere indiscernible
6. Can read beyond inadequate markings
7. You taught me everything indispensable
8. And when I'm done teaching my children
9. Now almost men
10. I fall down exhausted
11. Neural connections are born
12. Sleep is a complicated practice for wakefulness

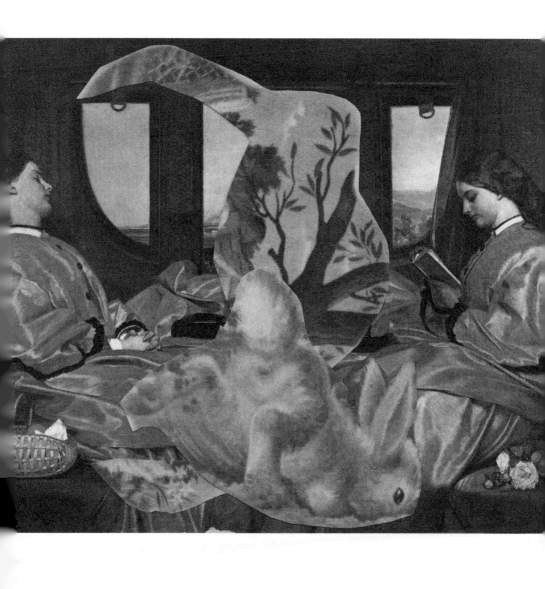

*What was it exactly we could not resist*

## 05.02.16

1. Everyone wants to meet on the day you've decided to be away

2. Bought a ticket for gone

3. Unmarked every square

4. You received no response for centuries until you decided to leave

5. How could you possibly miss the historic movement of bodies across lines

6. How many times will you hear those voices, live

7. How often will I embrace your breathing body

8. When do you first know you've begun to know

9. A person, a poem, a remedy for endings

10. Wasn't to be found in bundled cloth, woodsmoke or decoctions

11. Only song

12. Precariously among ruins

13. Of your otherwise fluent life

14. Still my strategy is not to look

15. Too closely at irresolvable mutiny

16. These documents speak to unwed futures

17. When we sign we are agreeing we've been born

18. We agree to go away eventually

19. We agree to wash premonition and give away brackish

20. Eventuality—never belonged to us

# 05.04.16

1. I worked to calm symptoms
2. But found they were persons
3. Too close to myself to name
4. So I combed names
5. The morning was leaking from a floor above
6. Through a light fixture onto the kitchen floor
7. When alone I found it necessary to lock the door
8. And when I walked it was not my decision
9. But the poem's prerogative
10. Passing mock lakes of pink petals
11. Pretending to cover ordinary pavement
12. Why do we find it difficult to discard unneeded garments
13. We hang momentary ideas in rows
14. Ready for any occasion
15. As if color itself were code
16. Or the desire to try on persons
17. In a closet that could be the public
18. Meeting possibility unborn
19. In sleep and in countless greetings
20. We learn to recognize ourselves
21. Absence can surround you
22. Conversations we don't have become most audible

23. Console yourself with the thought that repair

24. Will always be an aspect of the living

25. Be in beginning as long as you can

26. And then go back to the start

27. Even with the exact same circumstances

28. Like language repeating itself creating a desired effect

29. I love you—*I love you*—Iloveyou

30. See what I mean

31. I'm leaving

32. You'll never hear these words again

33. The world, or consciousness, is made of cellophane clouds

34. Bring your smart compass for pretension

35. Throw away everything but those pink petals

36. Already padding the ground

37. A leak is evidence that metal isn't the strongest

38. Power in mouth or hand

39. The strongest hour is now

40. Do I feed lamentation

41. Haven't I learned enough about emptiness

42. So this paying attention is useful after all

43. What was it exactly we could not resist

# 05.08.16

1. In the thick of colossal ancestral upshots
2. Where the Lower East Side is also Fairfax/Pico
3. You wonder why you would ever
4. Turn your head to follow a fast-moving
5. Fox on the edge of the word 'mother'
6. Cornering the sunroom in the morning
7. When two cities become one including
8. The childhoods of everyone standing in the vestibule
9. You had hoped you'd be invited up to meet her
10. Mother, a poet who lived in a palatial home
11. Inside a non-descript tenement building
12. Inside this diagram one Jewish neighborhood
13. Is uptown and impossible to carry. An unwieldy
14. Metal gong on a cart pushed through endless streets
15. Represents my mother's mortgage. Does the fox
16. Occur more often because she is worried
17. When he spoke the word 'mother' the fox appeared
18. Out the window as if speech brought forth apparition
19. Toads and crickets fell from his mouth
20. Jewels and blossoms disappeared when she died
21. Her mother saw no one, barely even her own daughter
22. We stood waiting in the near dark, disappointed

23. To remain below. Curious pink fringes hanging

24. From dismissive arms inform me

25. I'd never know, had never known her

26. The privacy inside every eye is inadmissible

27. Will you wake as expected, as planned and begin

28. The perilous ascent into your own radiance

29. I'm pleading as if supplication could

30. Forge the weight of your willingness

31. Into a deeply set body

32. Anandamaya kosha, remember

# 05.11.16

1. Gratitude, my sister, we often quarrel
2. Our kids almost the age at which we first met
3. I can't sleep with the door open, I wrote
4. And then I got up and closed the door
5. Morning sanctuary supports me even though I am not awake
6. Do you know morning sanctuary
7. Sitting beside me you took my hand, touched my hair
8. You didn't speak many eyes but you were blue
9. Silk, lemon, like indigo in a poem
10. A cat wearing a dress
11. An abstract luminous presence
12. I can no longer visit my grandmother's house
13. Not only is our invented childhood over
14. We've also spent the childhoods of our children
15. First *later* meant throwing everything in a closet, when they were small
16. Second, 'later' becomes a further projection
17. The desire for a time when everything is less devastating
18. Dear missing conspirators of birth and page
19. Assist us in finding words
20. Not to beautify, but to understand beyond surfaces

# 05.12.16

1. Mature now or wait until later
2. Look—your delusions are all in bloom
3. Every spring don't
4. Be duped by showy foliage
5. Still the same portals, chalices
6. Not necessarily doorways or entrances
7. A looming directory of inadmissible doom
8. Damp and forlorn, gloom in the brain
9. Or suddenly much too warm
10. As I approach the intersection I'm thinking—be alert
11. Let's roll this fog out and then walk on it
12. But as *non* went on-and-on and exhausted
13. By my own vicarious proclivities
14. Texts became endless dull birds
15. Larger than flight, furtive, preying on prone
16. Pronouncements. Never before have I seen
17. Scavengers so close though often circling above
18. Unimaginably slow, methodical, patient
19. Pecking head, nodding up and down
20. Calm now, pulling and ripping towns
21. What would happen if I approached
22. Would the slurred attack

23. Deferral is already dead. Must keep

24. Moving—half a stone well visible

25. Formerly obscured by shrubbery

26. This isn't a sign unless it means

27. Release, or the image of a large

28. Looming herd of mistakes

29. Remake myself, allowing

30. Dismemberment—feed on gone

# 05.14.16

1. Write a thank-you note to a terrible cocktail, a lack
2. Of confidence
3. Where lie the borders which when erased allow us to speak
4. It wasn't my fur to remove
5. Come closer—bring pelt and ink
6. Layers of worth I never knew I'd been missing
7. Came off in your felt-tipped dance, a photograph lost
8. Why regret the experiences we never had
9. As if they might have made edges or outlines visible
10. Summers spilled from lidless suns
11. You traveled. The taste of several languages
12. Appeared in your mouth
13. All I did not know came back to me threefold
14. Deafening gaze
15. Poverty gave me boundless appreciations
16. Wealth made me run faster
17. Until I lost count
18. Why is it that only when unwell do I allow
19. Myself to be giddily surrounded
20. By books saying 'yes'
21. Because the body is always first, demanding movement
22. I'm busy being available for others

23. Literally the exact same hours one is busy or happy

24. The other is lethargic and sad

25. The work of art every day is in how we fail

26. To avoid mirrors, open doors

27. Underwritten and barely budding, a field

## 05.19.16

1. Chekhov may have been a doctor
2. But he wasn't a mother *and* a writer
3. 'Mother' a job as taxing as doctor
4. Yet no pay
5. The hours are longer
6. Conditions may be hazardous
7. But even more precarious
8. Is your position in society
9. I made breakfast for one notion
10. While the other slept
11. Then took a walk and drove
12. Your thoughts to school
13. It feels like the dark ages
14. Even in the most liberated
15. Households where mothers slice dishes
16. From archaeological kitchens
17. And fainting fires into which we thrust
18. The simple privacy of eyes
19. We learn to speak singly and offer
20. Paralysis a place for recovery
21. A sound sewn into the hem of a frock

1. Because I'd been imprisoned
2. Call it a crash, a campaign, an echo
3. Best intentions rise early
4. Unending but unheard
5. Advocates for soporifics insist
6. Talks aim at doors
7. Grazing light
8. Eroding guardianship
9. With numbing frequency
10. Space isn't just an object
11. If I had nerves they were membranes
12. Dampness, culprits, easily rarefied
13. To insert yourself into emptiness
14. Requires air
15. Steps outside rigor
16. Spiders under chairs
17. What I learned at the cold cookout
18. Deliberately incinerated pyrotechnics
19. More authentic versions
20. Of our thoughts were not available
21. Why had we forgotten our idiocy
22. Intoning languages and locations

23. We knew near to nothing about

24. My list of objectives should come

25. Before wallowing

26. It's true you have to leave us

27. We will vacate all encumbered premises

28. But first learn the pleasures

29. Of dwelling in your own perfect form

30. And the imperative of inhabiting others

# COLLAGES

## ACKNOWLEDGMENTS

Some of these poems and collages originally appeared in the following publications: *Boston Review*, *Lute & Drum*, *A Perimeter*, *supplement*, and *Upstairs at Duroc*. Many thanks to Barbara Beck, Timothy Donnelly, Emily Goodman Means, Barbara Fischer, Binswanger Friedman, Stefania Heim, Pete Moore, Ariel Resnikoff, Carl Schlachte, Ken Taylor, and Orchid Tierney. The author is grateful for a Pew Fellowship and a MacDowell Colony residency which supported the writing of this book. Thank you: Lee Ann Brown, Forrest Gander, Edie Meidav, and Daniel Saldaña París for early readings. Tremendous thanks to everyone at Wave Books, especially Heidi Broadhead, Catherine Bresner, and Blyss Ervin. The title of this book is inspired by C. D. Wright's *Translations of the Gospel Back into Tongues*.